DATE DUE

GAYLORD			PRINTED IN U.S.A.

Joachim
Andersen

Recent Titles in
Bio-Bibliographies in Music

Gardner Read: A Bio-Bibliography
Mary Ann Dodd and Jayson Rod Engquist

Allen Sapp: A Bio-Bibliography
Alan Green

William Grant Still: A Bio-Bibliography
Judith Anne Still, Michael J. Dabrishus, and Carolyn L. Quin

Ross Lee Finney: A Bio-Bibliography
Susan Hayes Hitchens

Gerald Finzi: A Bio-Bibliography
John C. Dressler

Larry Sitsky: A Bio-Bibliography
Robyn Holmes, Patricia Shaw, and Peter Campbell

George Whitefield Chadwick: A Bio-Bibliography
Bill F. Faucett

William Schuman: A Bio-Bibliography
K. Gary Adams

Malcolm Arnold: A Bio-Bibliography
Stewart R. Craggs

Manuel de Falla: A Bio-Bibliography
Nancy Lee Harper

Elvis Costello: A Bio-Bibliography
James E. Perone

Carole King: A Bio-Bibliography
James E. Perone

Joachim Andersen

A Bio-Bibliography

Kyle J. Dzapo
Foreword by Walfrid Kujala

Bio-Bibliographies in Music, Number 73
Donald L. Hixon, *Series Adviser*

GREENWOOD PRESS
Westport, Connecticut • London

Library of Congress Cataloging-in-Publication Data

Dzapo, Kyle J.
    Joachim Andersen : a bio-bibliography / Kyle J. Dzapo ; foreword
by Walfrid Kujala.
      p.   cm.—(Bio-bibliographies in music, ISSN 0742–6968 ; no.
73)
    Includes bibliographical references and index.
    Discography: p.
    ISBN 0–313–30889–6 (alk. paper)
    1. Andersen, Joachim, 1847–1909—Bibliography. 2. Andersen,
Joachim, 1847–1909—Discography. I. Title. II. Series.
ML134.A59D9   1999
780′.92
[B]—dc21   99–30293

British Library Cataloguing in Publication Data is available.

Library of Congress Catalog Card Number: 99–30293
ISBN: 0–313–30889–6
ISSN: 0742–6968

First published in 1999

Greenwood Press, 88 Post Road West, Westport, CT 06881
An imprint of Greenwood Publishing Group, Inc.
www.greenwood.com

Printed in the United States of America

The paper used in this book complies with the
Permanent Paper Standard issued by the National
Information Standards Organization (Z39.48–1984).

10 9 8 7 6 5 4 3 2 1

To my parents, Marjorie and Carl Dzapo,
for their love, strength, and support of my musical career.

Contents

Foreword

Considering his far-reaching historical importance as a composer, flutist, conductor, and educator, it is surprising that there has been no previously published full-scale biography of Joachim Andersen. But Kyle Dzapo has now filled that void admirably with her *Joachim Andersen: A Bio-Bibliography*. Her painstakingly thorough research, which included examination of rare archival materials in Copenhagen, Berlin, New York, and Chicago, has resulted in a fascinating and engaging story of a most remarkable and indefatigable musician.

When it comes to the etude literature, Joachim Andersen is the undisputed "Chopin of the Flute." For more than a hundred years, this prolific Danish master's eight collections of flute etudes have been revered by flutists the world over. Ironically, the ubiquity of these etudes has in a way diverted too much attention from his substantial legacy of solo works for flute and piano (and flute and orchestra), some of which quite naturally exploit the virtuosic and bravura traits of the instrument, but many others of which highlight Andersen's impressive gift for melodic invention and varied harmonic style.

Dzapo's meticulously prepared listing in this volume of all of Andersen's works for flute, many with detailed commentary and analysis, should serve as a strong impetus for us performers to probe more deeply into his solo repertoire and revive some of his undeservedly neglected gems, and for publishers to reprint Andersen's out-of-print works so that they will be more widely accessible. This would go far towards enriching our relatively small romantic period repertoire.

Walfrid Kujala

Acknowledgments

One of the great pleasures in writing this book has been my association with Marianne Olesen, a wonderful Danish librarian who has conducted research and translated materials since I began work in Copenhagen in 1993. She has become a dear friend, and I thank her with all my heart for her fine work, energy, and love of this project.

The Bradley University Slane College of Communications and Fine Arts, Department of Music, Office of Research and Sponsored Programs, and Office of International Programs have generously supported my research.

Don Hixon, Pamela St. Clair, and Jane Lerner, editors at Greenwood Press, offered timely and valuable advice.

Dr. Richard Green, a member of my doctoral committee at Northwestern University, provided guidance during the early stages of this project and set a perfect example of academic excellence. Walfrid Kujala, whom I proudly call my teacher, has my deepest graditude, not only for writing the foreword, but also for his continuous help and guidance during the past ten years.

Anne Ørbæk Jensen and her colleagues at the Music History Museum and Carl Claudius Collection in Copenhagen welcomed me during three research trips and have graciously assisted me throughout the course of my work. I also thank Jutta March, Director of the National Institute for Music Research in Berlin and archivist of the Berlin Philharmonic Orchestra.

Walter Mayhall was among my first musical models and has guided my career and given me love and support since the beginning. His lively intellect and enthusiasm for scholarship inspired this book.

…and to the others who made all the difference.

Joachim Andersen (1847–1909), "Chopin of the Flute"
(Photographs from Victor Gandrup's Collection. Used with permission of the Musikhistorisk Museum og Carl Claudius Samling, Copenhagen, Denmark.)

In a striking departure from Tivoli Orchestra tradition, Maestro Joachim Andersen faced the musicians rather than the audience when conducting the more challenging and serious compositions he programmed for the ensemble. The conspicuous part down the back of his almost-bald head greatly amused both audience and critics, and became his trademark. (See pp. 23–24.)

Biography

Early Life and Career

In 1847, as western Europe delighted in the virtuosity of Franz Liszt and aspiring artists immersed themselves in the etudes and caprices of Chopin and Paganini, far north in Copenhagen, the next virtuoso, the "Chopin of the Flute," was born. He would become the most admired flutist of his day, compose the finest flute etudes ever written, and, with his colleagues, create one of the world's leading orchestras. He entered the world at the same time and in the same place as Tivoli Gardens, his career flourished as it flourished, and in later life, he became the tyrannical conductor of its orchestra and the most controversial and influential leader of Denmark's cultural life. Fiercely passionate and dedicated, he devoted his life to creating music of the highest order. He performed under Brahms, Grieg, Strauss, Tchaikovsky, and von Bülow, and then, after enduring personal tragedy, returned to Copenhagen to guide Danish musical life into the twentieth century.

A beautifully handwritten record completed at Garnisons Church confirms the birth of Carl Joachim Andersen: April 29, 1847, the first child of Christian Joachim Andersen (1816-99) and Caroline Frederikke Andkjær (1823-98), who had married on March 7, 1847. Three more children followed: Julie (born April 3, 1849), Vigo (born April 21, 1852), and Hilma (born August 25, 1855). The very poor young family lived at Rosengade 443 on the north side of Copenhagen during the children's early years. Christian, a native of Roskilde, Denmark, had been forced to provide for himself from an early age. (B42, p. 15) He enlisted in the Danish military musical corps as a young man and served as a rank-and-file soldier in the second brigade until 1864. (B34, p. 1) In that year, Prussia and Austria invaded Denmark in an attempt to take control of the duchies of Schleswig and Holstein. Following Denmark's defeat in the conflict, Andersen was discharged because of reductions in military expeditures. He was subsequently hired as a member of Hans Christian Lumbye's renowned Tivoli

Orchestra, where he remained until 1878. At the same time he taught flute and during later life, earned his living as a respected flute teacher. (B34, p. 1) His most gifted and well-known students were his two sons, Joachim and Vigo. Years later, Joachim dedicated his musically superb opus 15 collection of twenty-four etudes to "my beloved father and teacher C. J. Andersen."

On January 10, 1855, Joachim entered a neighborhood school for the children of military personnel. While a researcher's notes at the Music History Museum in Copenhagen suggest that he did not do well in school (Gandrup, B7), official records are missing from the city's archive. He began flute studies during the same year (B3, p. 1), using an eight-keyed wooden instrument, progressed rapidly, and at the age of thirteen performed a successful debut recital at the Casino Theater.   The Casino, developed by writer-architect Georg Carstensen, who had created Copenhagen's Tivoli Gardens in 1843, was originally intended to be a "Winter Tivoli." Unfortunately, it had a turbulent history because of poor management and its location in a dark corner of the city. (B28, p. 619) During the years 1848 to 1939, the Casino served primarily as a theater for the production of plays and operettas, but solo and chamber music recitals were also presented. Andersen not only performed his debut recital at the Casino, but also participated in chamber music concerts during subsequent years.

A short time after his debut, Andersen became principal flutist of the Musical Society's orchestra (*Musikforeningen*). Founded in 1836, the organization became a center of Copenhagen's concert life during the 1850s and 1860s when Niels Gade conducted the orchestra. Gade, an important nineteenth-century composer and conductor, served as assistant conductor of Felix Mendelssohn's Gewandhaus Orchestra in Leipzig, and, upon Mendelssohn's death in 1847, was appointed principal conductor of the orchestra. Because of the outbreak of war between Denmark and Prussia in 1848, however, Gade resigned his position and returned to Copenhagen where he devoted himself to the reorganization of the Musical Society. He established the Society's permanent orchestra which provided Andersen's early orchestral training.

Andersen's twenty-third year, 1869, proved to be a momentous one in the young musician's life. On September 14th, he married Emma Christina Jansson. Jansson, born December 13, 1846, in Karlstad, Sweden, was the daughter of a tailor named Johann Jansson (1816-57) and Malin Vikström (1819-died before 1860). (B26, p. 196) While the secrets of their marriage remain arcane, a sad series of events offers a rare glimpse into Joachim's personal life. His marriage to Emma did not last long, and by the beginning of November 1872, the two were living separately. In 1874, Emma and Joachim met with their respective clergy, the first step toward divorce. Emma cited Joachim's infidelity as her reason for wanting to end the marriage. She moved back to Stockholm, and the divorce was granted on February 15, 1878, following three years of required formal separation.

Just before their separation, the Andersens' only child was born. Ernst Gunner Joachim Andersen, born May 23, 1872, lived a short and pathetic life, dying at the age of twenty-seven. Like his father, he learned to play the flute (his death certificate lists his occupation as "Musician"), but he was forced to play everything by rote because he suffered from bleeding in the veins in his eyes which eventually led to his blindness. (Gandrup, B7) Joachim was granted custody of the child at the time of the divorce. As a young man intent on pursuing his musical career, however, he did not care for Ernst himself, but instead sent him to live with his own parents. Joachim left Copenhagen in 1878 to accept a position in St. Petersburg, leaving his young son behind. Ernst later married Thora Gunhild Zurzick (born April 27, 1867), and they lived, childless, in a dilapidated basement flat in Copenhagen until May 19, 1899, when he died of tuberculosis. No obituary recognized his life. According to the Probate Court, the two hundred crowns Ernst owned were used to pay burial expenses. It is not known whether Andersen or his ex-wife visited their child during the years when both lived out of the country. Joachim's only known public acknowledgment of his son was his dedication to Ernst of the fifth and sixth movements of his transcriptions *Schwedische Polska-Lieder*, op. 50, published in 1896.

Also in 1869, Andersen competed for and won a prestigious position with Copenhagen's Royal Orchestra. He began his employment, at an annual salary of twelve hundred crowns, on September 16, 1869, two days after his marriage. During the years 1869 to 1878, he performed with the orchestra and participated in chamber music concerts with colleagues. He undertook several solo concert tours to Sweden, Finland, and Holland during holiday breaks, and was granted two one-year leaves of absence (August 24, 1871, to August 15, 1872, and November 1, 1877, to November 6, 1878) to travel and perform. Then, like many of the finest Danish musicians of the time (including his brother Vigo and percussionist Victor Lanzky, who was Andersen's sister Hilma's husband), he left Denmark to pursue a better-paying orchestral position. Niels Friis, in his book *Det Kongelige Kapel* (The Royal Orchestra), relates:

> At the end of October in 1878, Joachim resigned, after actually performing only occasionally during the immediately preceding period. He had other irons in the fire. He was trying to launch a career as soloist, conductor, and teacher which he achieved when he returned to Denmark after many years abroad. His successor in the orchestra was his brother Vigo Andersen. He had been his substitute for a long time and probably in such an informal way that one never knew beforehand which one of the two brothers would play, except when Joachim was traveling, which was quite often toward the end. (B63, pp. 160-161)

The Berlin Years

St. Petersburg and Bilse's Orchestra

In late 1878, Andersen moved to St. Petersburg, where he spent three years playing in the Imperial Orchestra. Perhaps Wilhelm Ramsøe (1837-95), a Danish conductor who went to St. Petersburg in 1877, helped him secure the position. (Christiansen, B7) During this period, Andersen wrote a number of compositions and began to receive contracts with international publishing houses, including Max Leichssering of Hamburg and Rühle & Wendling of Leipzig. (B32, p. 4) Then, in 1881, he relocated to Berlin where he became principal flutist of the highly acclaimed Bilse Orchestra.

Benjamin Bilse (1816-1902), an important leader in Berlin's concert life for the seventeen years between 1867 and 1884, was a "stern, severe, white-bearded man" who served both as conductor and manager of his well-known orchestra. His ensemble, the finest of the four private orchestras in Berlin, maintained a demanding weekly schedule: Mondays, all-Wagner programs (Bilse was a fervent admirer); Tuesdays, works of the Classical period; Wednesdays, choral and other vocal music; Thursdays, music for dancing; Fridays, premieres and first performances (Bilse was also a well-known advocate of contemporary music); and Saturdays, light entertainment. (B58, p. 38) The orchestra was very successful, though perhaps because of this grueling schedule, it did not attain a distinguished level of performance.

A combination of events led to an upheaval in 1882. First came a guest appearance by the brilliantly trained Meiningen Orchestra conducted by Hans von Bülow. The small duchy of Saxe-Meiningen exercised undeniable influence on musical and dramatic performance at the time. Performances emanating from the duchy, including the appearance of the Meiningen Orchestra in Berlin, offered an unaccustomed quality which made a tremendous impression on members of the Bilse ensemble as well as the Berlin audience as a whole. Then, a short time later, Bilse planned a concert trip to Warsaw. Notoriously thrifty, he provided low wages and, as usual, fourth-class railway tickets for the musicians. The majority of the members refused the offer. Bilse, in turn, abruptly cancelled the trip, refused to extend the contracts of the dissenting musicians, and immediately put together a new orchestra for the subsequent season. (B56, p. 16) Andersen and fifty-three other musicians left Bilse's orchestra. Immediately winning a position in the Berlin Royal Opera orchestra, Andersen resigned after only a few months (B3, p. 1) and, with other former Bilse Orchestra members, began to work toward the formation of a new artistically excellent orchestra. The group formed an association which legally obligated them to stay together and began to give concerts independently in Berlin and other cities. (B56, p. 16) Needing a businessman who could advise them, organize and promote their ensemble, and help them to attract first-rate soloists and conductors, the musicians hired impresario Hermann Wolff.   Wolff was a tremendous asset. In addition to his care in publicizing the orchestra's concerts and making programming decisions, he also found a new concert hall for them— a converted roller-skating rink—which two of his business friends, Peter Landeker and Ludovic Sacerdoti, purchased a short time later.   This "Philharmonie" remained the Berlin Philharmonic's home until 1944 when it was destroyed in World War II.

The Berlin Philharmonic Orchestra

The Berlin Philharmonic Orchestra, founded May 1, 1882, began concertizing with tours in May and September-October 1882. The first winter season opened with their Berlin debut, a popular concert in the Philharmonie, on October 17, 1882. Popular concerts became a staple of the orchestra in these early years. Less formal than the "Philharmonic Concerts," but by no means lacking musical substance, they included food and beverages which audience members enjoyed at tables set up in the concert hall. Ludwig von Brenner, a protégé of Bilse and the orchestra's conductor, led this first concert. One of the soloists was Joachim Andersen, who performed the virtuosic *Le Carnaval Russe* of César Ciardi (presumably with his own cadenzas which were later published). A great honor for Andersen, this performance indicates that he was one of the most highly regarded musicians in the orchestra. An article in the *Berliner Tageblatt* of October 17, 1882, previewed the concert:

> The Philharmonic Orchestra, which returned from its brilliant tour on Sunday, begins its regular concerts today (four times weekly) in the Philharmonie under the leadership of Professor von Brenner.   The association of artists will introduce itself with a very interesting season. For example, tonight's concert will include three compositions which have never been performed in Berlin: the second Slavic Rhapsody of Dvorak, a Swedish dance for string orchestra by Gouvy, and the *Overture to King Manfred* by Karl Reinecke. (B55, I, p. 12)

And so it began. Andersen, thirty-five years old, hailed as "a brilliant flutist with uncommonly full tone and excellent technique" (B16, 18 October 1882), served as principal flutist during the orchestra's first eleven years. An extremely dedicated and hard-working musician, he composed, conducted, taught, and served as soloist during these years, in addition to meeting the rigorous demands of the Philharmonic's schedule. In 1890-91, for example, the orchestra played 382 concerts. Eleven of these were designated "Philharmonic Concerts," and were the main events of Berlin's musical season. The other 371 concerts included:

> 86 popular concerts (virtually every Sunday, Tuesday, and Wednesday evening between October 5, 1890, and April 29, 1891),
> 62 concerts contracted by soloists, music schools, choral societies, charitable organizations (as fundraisers for their causes), and a few royal/noble/wealthy families,
> 7 tour concerts, and
> 216 spa concerts at Scheveningen, Holland (twice daily from June 15 through September 30, 1891).

Andersen performed as soloist at the Philharmonic's popular concerts many times each year. During the 1887-88 season in Berlin, he served as soloist no fewer than seventeen times, performing thirteen different compositions:

1	*L'Illusion, Fantasie für Flöte* by Fürstenau (three performances)
2	*Variations für Flöte über ein schwedisches Volkslied*, op. 35, by Andersen
3	Concerto No. 2 in D Major, K. 314, by Mozart
4	*Le Carnaval Russe* by Ciardi (three performances, the second by popular demand)
5 & 6*	"Scène orientale" and "Capricio orientale" by Bird
7 & 8*	"Andante" by Molique and "Tarantelle" by Reicherdt
9	*Andante und Variationen für Violine, Viola, und Flöte aus der Serenade*, op. 25, by Beethoven
10 & 11*	No. 4 and 5 from the Ballet "Die Geschöpfe des Prometheus" by Beethoven (by popular demand)
12	*Tarantella für Flöte und Clarinette* by Saint-Saëns (four performances)
13	*Fantasie über Themen aus Mozart's "Don Juan"* by Dunkler
	* Each of these pairs was featured in one performance.

The greatest honor for a Philharmonic musician was to be selected as a soloist for one of the "Philharmonic Concerts." During Andersen's eleven years with the orchestra (from its founding on May 1, 1882, until his resignation April 30, 1893), the ensemble performed 137 of these concerts. Only eight did not feature a soloist (or multiple soloists). The remaining 129 included soloists as follows:

> 61 concerts with piano soloists
> 51 concerts with vocal soloist(s) and/or chorus(es)

49	concerts with violin soloists
10	concerts with cello soloists
1	concert with a viola soloist
_3_	concerts with wind (woodwind or brass) soloists
175	soloists (exceeds the total of 129 concerts because many included a singer and a pianist in separate works or several soloists in a single work)

It seems likely that Joachim Andersen was the intended soloist for all three of the 137 "Philharmonic Concerts" that featured winds during his tenure with the orchestra. He performed Mozart's Concerto in D Major, K. 314, on March 7, 1884. On January 23, 1888, he and principal clarinetist Carl Esberger performed Saint-Saëns' *Tarantella for Flute, Clarinet, and Orchestra.* And, although Wilhelm Tieftrunk, principal flutist of the Hamburg Symphony Orchestra, was featured in a "Philharmonic Concert" on March 28, 1892, this solo performance had probably also been intended for Andersen, and Tieftrunk appeared only as a substitute. Program announcements reveal that Andersen was scheduled to perform J. S. Bach's Suite in B Minor on December 7, 1891. But his performance had to be postponed because of illness, as a letter from Hans von Bülow to Andersen, dated December 5, 1891, confirms:

> Most Honorable Colleague!
> I received your both kind and pathetic letter from Hamburg a few minutes ago. Let me express to you my deepest compassion for your suffering (Did it appear to me that the Philharmonic Orchestra had but one eye at the rehearsal yesterday?), and send my most heartfelt wishes for a speedy recovery.
> Naturally we shall delay the performance of Bach's Suite for the flute. And even though your students gave you much honor in Brahms's Chaconne (in 3/2), the master himself would surely miss your poetic and soulful interpretation as much as does my humble self.
> Would you please be good enough to show up at the greenroom at least? A concert conducted by me and without your presence seems almost unthinkable.

In a hurry
Yours respectfully,
H. v. Bülow
Berlin, Saturday morning
5. Dec. 91. (B19, 22 February 1894)

The concert, it seems, was postponed for four months, and because Andersen was still unable to play, Tieftrunk stepped in and performed the Suite.

It remains a remarkable testament to Andersen's skill as a performer that he was the only wind player in the Philharmonic, and probably the only wind player in the world, selected to perform a solo concerto on a "Philharmonic Concert" during these years. Contemporary concert reviews confirm in what high regard his artistry was held. Critics repeatedly wrote of his beautiful tone and phenomenal technique. Following the January 23, 1888, "Philharmonic Concert" featuring the Saint-Saëns *Tarantella for Flute, Clarinet, and Orchestra* and Richard Strauss's *Aus Italien*, conducted by its composer, a reviewer for the *Vössische Zeitung* offered this critique:

> ...The Tarantella for flute and clarinet with orchestra by Saint-Saëns [was] a slick work which made a unique impression more through its juxtaposition of the two solo instruments than through its musical substance. The composition was realized with tonal beauty, perfect virtuosity, and lively expression by Messrs. Andersen and Esberger, members of the Philharmonic Orchestra... (B21, 24 January 1888)

And Franz Schnedler-Petersen, a violin student at the Berlin Hochschule, a colleague in the Philharmonic, and later Andersen's concertmaster and successor as conductor of Copenhagen's Palace Concerts and Tivoli Orchestra, wrote the following:

> During my years of study in Berlin, I had rich opportunities to know him as a wonderful flutist with a beautiful, velvet tone. This, in addition to his musicality, I remember as being absolutely incomparable, and I still remember [more than fifty years later] how wonderfully he played a concerto by Spohr in the Philharmonie. (B70, p. 93)

In 1885, Andersen was appointed assistant conductor of the Philharmonic. His primary responsibility was to conduct daily summer concerts at the orchestra's summer home, a seaside spa in the small Dutch town of Scheveningen. The concerts provided an excellent forum for Andersen to develop his conducting skills. (B35, p. 31) He conducted a three o'clock concert each afternoon, with the program generally consisting of six light classical works. The repertoire included Rossini, Mozart, and Mendelssohn overtures, Johann Strauss waltzes, and other short works by eighteenth- and nineteenth-century composers such as Haydn, Gade, Reinecke, Schumann, Bizet, Delibes, and Saint-Saëns. Following his death, Andersen's widow, Sarah Dana Watson

Andersen, an employee of the Music Division of the New York Public Library, donated twenty-four hundred concert programs to the library including many from Scheveningen.

In addition to conducting the afternoon concerts, Andersen performed in the orchestra during the evening concerts, performances which frequently included his appearance as a soloist. He played such works as the Mozart flute concerti, the *Carnival of Venice* by Jules Demerssemann, *Le Carnaval Russe* by César Ciardi, and several of his own compositions: *Wien Neerlands Bloed*, op. 35, *Allegro Militaire*, op. 48, *Pirun Polska*, op. 49, "La Résignation" of op. 22, and the "Babillard" of op. 24. These selections, largely nineteenth-century showpieces, attest to Andersen's extraordinary technical command of the instrument. His mastery of these works is especially remarkable given the difficulty of performing them on the eight-keyed wooden instrument which he used throughout his career.

The Philharmonic's second summer season in Scheveningen was cut short because of a fire which occurred at the spa on September 1, 1886. Much of Andersen's music as well the musicians' instruments (purchased for them by the eleemosynary Philharmonic Society the previous year) burned, and while the Dutch people took up a collection to help the musicians regain some of their losses, it was nevertheless a disaster for the ensemble.

Andersen continued to teach during these busy years. Among his most famous students were Jay Plowe (1870-1943), Ary van Leeuwen (1875-1953), and Emil Prill (1867-1940). Plowe, an American flutist, performed in the Berlin Royal Opera orchestra, then returned to the United States where he became principal flutist of the Los Angeles Philharmonic. In 1899, he traveled to Copenhagen where, on September 6th, he appeared as soloist with the Tivoli Orchestra under Andersen's baton. How touching it must have been for the teacher and student to reunite, and for Andersen to enjoy a performance of his *Deuxième Impromptu*, op. 54, and the première of another of his works, titled *Caprice*.

Emil Prill studied at the Berlin Hochschule between 1882 and 1884. He became principal flutist of the Hamburg Philharmonic Orchestra in 1889 and later served as principal flutist of the Berlin Royal Opera orchestra and teacher at the Berlin Hochschule. Like the other successful Andersen students, Prill was a featured soloist on Tivoli Orchestra programs conducted by Andersen. In August of 1901, among other works, Prill performed Andersen's *Concertstück*, op. 3, and *Variations Drolatiques*, op. 26. Andersen dedicated his *Introduction et Caprice sur des Airs Hongroises*, op. 58, to Prill.

Ary van Leeuwen began studies with Andersen in Scheveningen, then moved to Berlin because, in his words, Andersen "in his enthusiasm for me got my father's permission to take me to Berlin to complete my studies with him." (B39, p. 180) Van Leeuwen served as principal flutist of the Berlin Philharmonic

Orchestra between 1897 and 1901, and later became principal flutist of the Imperial Opera in Vienna under Gustav Mahler. In late June of 1905, he traveled to Copenhagen to perform as a soloist on three Tivoli Orchestra programs under Andersen's baton. He, too, honored his teacher by performing *Fantaisie Caractéristique*, op. 16, "Intermezzo," op. 51, no. 2, and "Scherzino," op. 55, no. 6, the latter two with piano accompaniment.

On June 2, 1891, thirteen years after the end of his first marriage, Andersen married for the second time. This union appears to have been a happier one, lasting almost eighteen years until his death in 1909. His bride, Sarah ("Sally") Dana Watson, born in New York on August 4, 1855, was a fine pianist who studied with the renowned Franz Xaver Scharwenka in Berlin. (Gandrup, B7) Described as "an unusually kind American lady, who is as smiling as her husband is serious" (B20, 27 January 1898), she and Joachim were "devout party-goers who moved among the highest society." (B9) A devoted partner, Sally collected programs, notes, and newspaper articles of her husband's performances throughout Europe, then carefully preserved them in large scrapbooks. The romantic distinction of this collection lies in her personal, handwritten comments. She saved each program which Andersen conducted, and corrected those in which he served as a last-minute substitute for another conductor, indicated the weather on summer Scheveningen concert programs, and occasionally included other details, poignantly writing "the last," for example, following Andersen's final concert in 1909. Shortly after her husband's death, Sally returned to New York, obtained a position at the New York Public Library, and donated her scrapbooks as well as first-edition copies of Andersen's music to the library. She was employed for four-and-a-half years, resigning on April 30, 1915. (B15) The last extant correspondence from Sally, a postcard sent from New York to the Wilhelm Hansen Publishing Company in Copenhagen on June 12, 1928, acknowledged receipt of radio royalty checks. (B14)

Debilitating Paralysis

Late in 1891 Andersen developed a tongue paralysis which forced him to resign his position with the Berlin Philharmonic and give up his career as a performing flutist. It was the onset of this affliction which caused the cancellation of his solo appearance at the December 7, 1891, "Philharmonic Concert." Andersen continued to play as much as possible, but by the summer of 1892, he was performing very little. During the summer of 1891, for example, he presented solo works at ten concerts. Only rarely did another flutist perform as a soloist with the orchestra. During the summer of 1892, however, nine flute solo pieces were performed. Andersen appeared as soloist in only one performance, and there were few subsequent performances of any kind in which he participated as a flutist.

While no definitive information is available regarding the cause of Andersen's illness, it is mentioned in several sources. An article in the *Politiken*, one of Copenhagen's daily newspapers, of January 27, 1898, reported simply that the tongue disease was caused by "exhaustion." (B20, 27 January 1898) Andersen confirmed this explanation without elaboration in his *curriculum vitae* of 1905. (B3) Leonardo De Lorenzo, a noted flutist during the mid-twentieth century and the author of *My Complete Story of the Flute*, later speculated about a possible cause for the exhaustion:

> Andersen who, by the way, was as much against double tonguing as he was antagonistic to the Boehm flute, said that the real staccato on the flute should be single tonguing. He therefore, while his contemporaries were discussing or studying the possibilities of the new flute, practiced so much single tonguing staccato, to prove his theory that it could be done, that he injured the tip of his tongue and, in the last years of his life, could not play at all! (B39, p. 322)

No other sources corroborate this account.

More plausible is the argument that Andersen's tongue paralysis was a symptom of syphilis. While his death certificate cites "aorta aneurysma" (stroke) as the cause of death, the duration of his degeneration as well as the symptoms exhibited during his final years are consistent with deterioration caused by syphilis rather than an acute attack such as a stroke.

References to the paralysis were made in several letters written to Andersen by Paul Taffanel, principal flutist of the Paris Opera between 1876 and 1890 and flute professor at the Paris Conservatory between 1893 and 1908. One of the letters from Taffanel, dated Paris, May 5, 1895, began:

> My dear friend
> It has been a long time since I've had news from you...
> I learned indirectly that the state of your health had worried your friends, but I had reason to believe that you had promptly recovered because I have been able to notice with satisfaction that you were continuing to enrich the flutist's library with your always charming and distinctive compositions... (B8)

A subsequent letter, dated Paris, May 28, 1895, opened this way:

My dear Andersen!

I was saddened by your letter in which you told me that you could no longer perform in public. This must be very frustrating for you. I hope that you don't despair about recovering this ability to play staccato which has left you these past years.—At your age such misfortunes can only be temporary, particularly because your general health is good.—It seems to me that some very progressive and very systematic exercises should, with a lot of care and time, help you to recover your former skill.—I've had, myself, during an entire year, a deficiency of the lips that prevented me from going higher than e^3.—I thought I could never recover my ability which nevertheless came back one day as before.—I hope that it will be the same for you... (B8)

In contrast to the promise of Taffanel's encouraging testimonial, Andersen's performing ability never completely returned. He had resigned his position with the Berlin Philharmonic two years earlier on April 30, 1893 (B55, I, p. 3), causing von Bülow to comment: "When he left us, the sun set on the Berlin Philharmonic Orchestra." (Gandrup, B7) He returned to Copenhagen where he devoted the rest of his career to composing and conducting. Upon his departure, the Board of Directors of the spa in Scheveningen presented Andersen with an ornate ivory baton decorated with instruments and inscribed with the dates 1885-1892. Andersen's widow donated this baton to the Music History Museum and Carl Claudius Collection in Copenhagen shortly after her husband's death.

Hans von Bülow's support during this tragic period was recounted in a lengthy article, dated February 22, 1894, in the *Dannebrog*, a daily Copenhagen newspaper which frequently published articles about Andersen and always treated him favorably:

Hans von Bülow and Joachim Andersen

Hans von Bülow, who died a few days ago [February 12, 1894], greatly esteemed Joachim Andersen as a flutist and conductor.

When Andersen suffered a severe tongue disease toward the end of 1891, and for a long time had to give up his job as a flutist, he wrote Hans von Bülow a letter and asked for advice. A short time later, he received... [a] reply in an envelope addressed as follows: Mr. Joachim Andersen, the genuine expert of music... [Von Bülow's letter is printed on page seven.]

Later, when Andersen had decided to become a conductor, he wrote to Bülow for a letter of recommendation, and received the following letter from the famous musician:

Hamburg, 2 April 1893.
Honorable colleague!

I am in debt to you for the letter you sent me on November 3rd last year! However disabled I still feel: on March 13 [the date von Bülow conducted the last concert of the Berlin Philharmonic's season] only the ghost of my former fame, brightened by the spirit of the orchestra in which there is also an echo of you, personified by your student, led to a beautiful result—so it is that I wish my weakness may soon come to an end so that I can prove useful to your plans which have my sincere admiration and sympathy.

But how can this be realized?   Shall I sign a "testimony"? It seems to me more a matter of getting you a dignified position among gentlemen. Where? How? In a smaller town in the rural area at a beach spa?—that is no place for you. If you had something in mind, then I should do my best—if ever I again come into a position of playing the piano under your direction. Yet is it more correct and simple that I stick to your draft and write a "testimony" in the usual form in which these kinds of papers are demanded and delivered? If I can do it better, according to your wishes, please let me know, and please forgive me for my failures.

I did it of a good will.
H. v. Bülow

Bülow's letter of recommendation:

Mr. Joachim Andersen, until last year principal flutist of the Berlin Philharmonic Orchestra, and as it is generally known, a flute virtuoso, composer, teacher, and assistant conductor, is one of the gems of this organization. Mr. Andersen honors the undersigned by requesting from him a statement regarding his conducting abilities. The undersigned has rarely been so vigorously filled with the wish of being able to assist an artist so manifoldly educated, theoretically as well as practically. Besides, he knows Mr. Andersen very well as an orchestra leader since he has not often missed an afternoon concert in Scheveningen, has enjoyed his fine way of conducting various pieces, and has always admired his dignified approach.

Hamburg, end of March, 1893.

Anyone who has met Hans von Bülow knows that such a letter of recommendation has great influence. (B19, 22 February 1894)

In spite of von Bülow's glowing letter (which ironically was written five months after Andersen's correspondence to him), there are no indications that he or the Philharmonic administration helped Andersen to gain another conducting position or invited him to continue conducting after the advent of symptoms of his disease. Andersen had occasionally conducted popular concerts during the orchestra's winter seasons, but he was not called upon so often as the other assistant conductors. And, although he was associated with the Philharmonic until April 1893, he did not conduct more frequently during the final year of his tenure when he could not play.

By the time he tendered his resignation and returned to Copenhagen, Andersen had completed most of his compositions. A delightfully revealing reference found, oddly enough, on a postcard related that "during his years in Berlin, he used to sit at the very back of a bar and write most of his music for flute and piano." (Christiansen, B7, p. 5) By 1893, many of Andersen's etude collections were already being used in the most prominent music schools in Berlin, Leipzig, Dresden, Hamburg, Vienna, Weimar, St. Petersburg, Moscow, Paris, Brussels, the Hague, and Turin. He became known as the "Chopin of the Flute" in Paris, and Taffanel wrote: "As soon as I started in the position [Professor of Flute, Paris Conservatory], my first concern was to introduce into my teaching your valuable etudes as well as your other compositions... The study of your works pleases my young students, and it is your name that is the 'big favorite' in my class..." (B8) Already in February of 1894, the *Dannebrog* reported: "Joachim Andersen's fame as a composer of flute music is well known, and almost all flutists keep his music among their standard pieces." (B19, 12 February 1894) In the notes to his recording, *Morceaux pour la Flûte avec accompagnement de Piano par Joachim Andersen*, Toke Lund Christiansen related:

Marcel Moyse told me the moving story that when Joachim Andersen came to Paris in 1904 (where Moyse studied in Taffanel's class at the Conservatoire Superieur de Paris), Taffanel played the big G major etude from opus 15 [#3] so wonderfully that Andersen commented: *"I had no idea I had written something that beautiful!"* (B32, p. 4)

Adolph Hennebains (1862-1914), Taffanel's successor as Professor of Flute at the Paris Conservatory, also used the etudes extensively in his classes and once stated, "Truly blessed are the pianists with Chopin's etudes while we flutists are uniquely privileged to have Andersen's etudes." (B34, p. 1) In addition, Andersen's *Concertstück*, op. 3, and his *Deuxième Morceau de Concert*, op. 61, were both selected by Taffanel to be examination pieces for the Conservatory's flute *concours*.

Return to Copenhagen

The Palace Concerts, The Lübeck Exhibition, and Vigo Andersen's Death

Andersen's first major venture after returning to Copenhagen was the initiation of a new series of orchestral concerts, later called the Palace Concerts. The purpose of these concerts, according to Anton Hansen, a trombonist in the orchestra, was "to make accessible to the common people of society, for an inexpensive fee, the masterpieces of music in as good a performance as allowed by the conditions." (B69, p. 129)   The concerts began experimentally at the Odd-Fellow Palace in Copenhagen on February 22, 1894.   On the eve of the inaugural concert, the *Politiken* included an article designed to reintroduce Andersen to the people of Copenhagen:

> Young music-lovers will not recall Joachim Andersen's flute playing which is described by those who remember with high praise.   It has been more than a generation since he left the Royal Orchestra and traveled through Sweden and Finland to St. Petersburg.   Later he lived for twelve or thirteen years in Berlin.
> Now he returns to Copenhagen with a reputation as a soloist throughout Europe and lesser fame as a conductor, though not less well-deserved.
> Who could doubt that the Copenhagen musical audience will welcome our great fellow-citizen on Thursday night.
> —We introduce the "foreign" citizen of Copenhagen to our readers:
> He is a sturdy, upright person of more than medium height, whose well-dressed manner is in harmony with his correct man-of-the-world attitude.   His face radiates a good-natured temperament, shown by the almost hidden little smile

behind an enormous mustache. In his wide-open blue eyes one sees an energetic look. He speaks a remarkably correct Danish with a vague German accent.

After a bit of small talk about the troublesome journey, concerts ahead and other matters, we ask Joachim Andersen for his opinion on the difference between musical life in Berlin and Copenhagen.

—"I've been thinking about it," he exclaims vigorously. "We should have something besides theater and music halls. People want to spend the evening dining and drinking, and I believe that the Copenhagen audience is big enough to support such a place. The Odd-Fellow Palace would be fine for this kind of winter Tivoli concert.

—"And what an educating effect such a place could have... on the public, the musicians, young conductors and composers—and the old ones as well—who have difficulty getting their works performed. What a forum for the young musicians and singers who long for an understanding audience.

—"But only God knows if there is enough initiative to start such an institution," sighs Mr. Andersen.

—"Couldn't you lead this, sir?" we asked.

—"My greatest wish. This is exactly what I want, either here or somewhere else. But I cannot do it alone, of course. And first we will have to see how my symphony concerts go."

And then we left Mr. Joachim Andersen.

On Thursday the public can judge this winter's "Balduin Dahl."

[Balduin Dahl was a former conductor of the Tivoli Orchestra.]

(B20, 21 February 1894)

A review in the *Politiken*   (February 23, 1894) of Andersen's first concert told of its enormous success:

Joachim Andersen's First Symphony Concert

The full house, and the great applause that followed each of the pieces showed that Mr. Joachim Andersen has succeeded in achieving the Berlin Philharmonic Orchestra's standard in his hometown. And, without a doubt, he is the man for this job. Good-looking and popular—with his marvelous Berlin parting of hair down the back of his head and

a white glove on his left hand—he combines his talents as
conductor and musician... (B20, 23 February 1894)

A second, equally successful concert was presented three weeks later. Ludwig
Bleuer, concertmaster of the Berlin Philharmonic Orchestra, was the soloist and
performed Beethoven's D-Major Violin Concerto.

Encouraged by the success of these initial concerts, an ongoing series
was established beginning a year-and-a-half later (October 30, 1895), with an all-
Wagner program. The Palace Concerts received administrative help from the
Wilhelm Hansen Publishing House and financial support from the city, the
Danish government, and private donors. (B70, p. 98) At first, the concerts took
place on Thursday evenings and, at a less expensive price, on Sunday afternoons.
But because the audience was not large enough to support two performances each
week, organizers subsequently decided to present only one weekly concert. These
were performed on Sunday afternoons throughout the winter. The budget
permitted only one two-hour rehearsal for each concert. For this reason, and
because the orchestra used the same personnel as the summer Tivoli Orchestra,
both organizations played the same repertoire during the years that Andersen
conducted the two ensembles. (B70, pp. 98-99) In his book, *Træk Af Dansk
Musiklivs Historie M. M.*, Lars Børge Fabricius quotes Franz Schnedler-
Petersen, Andersen's concertmaster at the time, as saying that each orchestra
member was paid nine crowns per week to perform both the rehearsal and concert
during the first season. At the end of the season, however, only seven-and-a-half
crowns were left as payment for Andersen. (B61, p. 391)

Andersen's initiation of these concerts in 1894 proved a major
contribution to Danish musical life. During subsequent years, twenty concerts
were presented each season, and they became well known and increasingly
popular. The *Politiken* reported that success was due in part to the fact that
Andersen "was a wise idealist who knew how to attract his audience, what he
could offer, and what he had to leave out." (B20, 8 May 1909) The Palace
Concerts continued until 1931, twenty-two years after Andersen's death, when it
is said that "people began to prefer the new technical wonder, the radio."
(Gandrup, B7)

During the summer of 1895, Andersen conducted a special series of
orchestra concerts in Lübeck, a city on the Baltic coast of Germany which was
the site of that year's German-Nordic Exhibition of Trade and Industry. In his
handwritten *curriculum vitae* of 1905, Andersen wrote:

Warmly recommended by Dr. Hans von Bülow, Dr. Joseph
Joachim, Dr. Frederik Wüllner, Dr. Edvard Grieg and others, I
was chosen after a competition to lead an orchestra of 63
musicians... As a reward I received a gold medal saying: 'For

> self-sacrificing deeds and excellent skills as conductor of the
> great exhibition orchestra throughout the period of the
> exhibition.' (B3, p. 2)

The *Dannebrog* proclaimed Andersen "a great success" and reported on a special concert he arranged for his wife's birthday, during which "Miss Fanny Christensen played three pieces composed by the master himself." (B19, 10 August 1895) Lübeck was Andersen's last major conducting engagement outside of Copenhagen, though the *Dannebrog* had erroneously reported earlier in the spring that the Board of Directors of the Cincinnati Symphony had offered him a conducting position to begin the following winter. (B19, 9 May 1895)

During the winter preceding the Lübeck Exhibition, Andersen suffered the loss of his younger brother, Vigo (1852-95). Vigo had succeeded Joachim as a flutist in the Royal Orchestra in Copenhagen, and then, like many of the finest musicians in Denmark, had left in pursuit of a better paying position abroad. He received a one-year leave of absence on September 1, 1889, left his wife, children, and debts, and moved to the United States. He never returned to Copenhagen and was dismissed from the Royal Orchestra on December 31, 1890. After performing with the 22nd Regiment Band in New York, Vigo became a founding member and the principal flutist of the Chicago Orchestra (later known as the Theodore Thomas Orchestra, the predecessor of the Chicago Symphony Orchestra), a position he held until his shocking and spectacular suicide in 1895 at the age of forty-two.

Vigo was a prominent member of Thomas' orchestra from its inception in 1891, and one of its most frequent soloists. During the orchestra's first season, he and principal clarinetist, Joseph Schreurs, performed the Saint-Saëns *Tarantella for Flute, Clarinet, and Orchestra* at the orchestra's concert hall (the Auditorium) on January 22 and 23, 1892, and in concerts in Joliet and Bloomington, Illinois;   Lafayette, Indiana;   LaCrosse and Milwaukee, Wisconsin; St. Louis, Missouri; Louisville, Kentucky; and Omaha, Nebraska. Vigo Andersen was also the featured soloist during the orchestra's second season, performing his brother's composition, *Fantasia for Flute on the Dutch National Hymn,* op. 35, and during its third when he performed J. S. Bach's Suite No. 2 in B Minor. During his years in Chicago, Andersen also served on the faculty of the Columbian College of Music, a school located near the Auditorium where a number of Chicago Orchestra members taught.

During the fourth season, advertisements in the concert programs announced that Vigo Andersen would again solo with the orchestra. Weeks before this was to occur, however, the renowned flutist committed suicide. Ironically, this dramatic event gave him his greatest fame. An article in the *Chicago Daily Tribune* of January 30, 1895, related the story:

SUICIDE AT A SOIREE
PROF. VIGO ANDERSEN, THE FLUTIST, ABRUPTLY TAKES HIS LIFE.

Prof. Vigo Andersen... a prominent member of Theodore Thomas' Orchestra, made a dramatic ending to his somewhat eventful life last night.   He called together practically all his friends and gave them a grand musical entertainment. Then he shot himself through the head.

The suicide occurred at 10:20 o'clock at No. 347 Elm Street, where Mr. Andersen was living.   One of the invited guests was Miss Frances Streigel, No. 410 Dearborn Avenue. Andersen killed himself virtually at her feet.   Many of his acquaintances declare Andersen was the fiancé of Miss Streigel, but her friends deny this.

Many motives are assigned for the suicide. The true one seems to be a desire to make a dramatic exit after a combination of marital troubles...

Vigo Andersen was one of the most brilliant flutists in the world.   Firm, precise, reliable, always the thorough artist in all that he undertook, his loss is a severe one to the musical world, and in especial to Chicago in his connection with the Chicago Orchestra.   In addition to his eminent accomplishments as soloist, he wrote a number of excellent compositions for flute.

His appearances as soloist with the orchestra, both at the Auditorium and Exposition concerts, were numerous. Never upon any occasion did he fall short in the most exacting finish and excellence, and his place in the esteem of concert audiences was absolutely unquestioned... (B18, 30 January 1895)

According to Victor Gandrup, who was an avid collector of materials about Danish musical life, Joachim Andersen greatly admired his brother both as a man and as a musician. "Whenever Vigo was mentioned, Joachim praised him 'to the skies' as a flutist and stressed his own inferiority to his brother.   And his eyes welled up with tears if the subject was talked about too much. Remembering his brother always overwhelmed him." (Gandrup, B7)   Joachim, who had earlier dedicated his *Fantaisie Caractéristique*, op. 16, to Vigo, also composed *The School of Virtuosity, 24 Grand Studies for Flute*, op. 60, for his brother. The most technically demanding etudes of Andersen's eight collections, opus 60 attests to the composer's high regard for Vigo's superb musical capability.

The Orchestra School

During the next year, Joachim Andersen began a new venture.   On September 15, 1896, he opened an "Orchestra School."   An article in the *Dannebrog* of August 26, 1896, explained Andersen's purpose in starting the school:

> Until now, there has been little opportunity for a young [inexperienced] musician to become a member of a [paid] orchestra. The orchestras have been only too keen to augment their ranks [with unpaid amateurs]. But the founding of the orchestra union has made it more difficult for orchestras to use unpaid players. [Now that Joachim Andersen had to pay virtually all his musicians, he] was often obliged to reject young players [whom he might have accepted as volunteers, but whose skills did not warrant payment]. It became clear to him that young people needed a place to practice ensemble playing and obtain the skills required by orchestras that did not have much time for rehearsal. (B19, 26 August 1896)

Although Andersen's primary goal was to educate young musicians in the art of ensemble playing, the school offered music history classes designed "to add understanding and knowledge of classic and modern orchestral repertoire." (B9) Classes met twice a week with strict attendance policies, and scholarships were provided for needy students.

Students entering the program were required to have at least two years of instrumental experience and were expected to commit to at least four months of participation at a cost of approximately five crowns per month.   A student who successfully completed the entire three-year course of study could, "if he is considered mature and skilled, achieve a certificate of diligence and competence." (B9) One hundred twenty-four students enrolled in the school during its first five years; thirty passed the three-year course and achieved positions in orchestras and military bands. (B9)

During the early years, Andersen rented a school gym, located at Store Kongensgade 31, for rehearsals and classes.   The Orchestra School moved to Vestre Boulevard 22 in 1897, then to the Danish Royal Conservatory of Music on Vestre Boulevard in 1905, where it provided the Conservatory's first courses in ensemble playing. The Orchestra School's concerts were generally performed at the Odd-Fellow Palace. The first one occurred May 30, 1897, with a program of seven compositions including Mozart's *Overture to Don Giovanni*, Johan Svendsen's *Andante Funebre* and Bernhard Molique's "Andante," featuring Orchestra School flutist Fanny Christensen.

The orchestra consisted of twenty-six members with the following instrumentation: 8 first violins, 5 second violins, 2 violas, 1 cello, 1 bass, 2 flutes, 1 oboe, 1 clarinet, 2 horns, 2 trumpets, and 1 trombone. During subsequent years, the enrollment steadily increased. By the 1903-04 season, there were forty-nine members, including 13 first violins, 12 second violins, 4 violas, 4 cellos, 1 bass, 3 flutes, 3 clarinets, 2 bassoons, 3 horns, 2 trumpets, and 2 trombones, and by Andersen's twelfth season (1907-08), sixty-six students were enrolled in the program.

During Andersen's tenure, a number of outstanding flutists participated in the Orchestra School: Robert Enevoldsen, who later became principal flutist of the Palace orchestra; Christian Agerup, who performed "Ecossais" from Andersen's *Fantaisies Nationales*, op. 59, on an Orchestra School program of March 10, 1901, and later became second flutist of the Palace orchestra; Johannes Ahlquist, who performed Andersen's "Legende," op. 55, no. 5, and "Babillard," op. 24, no. 6, on an Orchestra School program on May 8, 1904; and Fanny Christensen, who, in addition to performing on the first Orchestra School program in 1897, had also presented solo works with the Tivoli Orchestra in April of 1893, at the 1895 Exhibition in Lübeck under Andersen's baton, and on another Orchestra School program on February 20, 1898. Andersen dedicated the first and second of his six transcriptions *Schwedische Polska-Lieder*, op. 50, to Christensen.

The Tivoli Orchestra

Andersen's most significant conducting position began in 1898 when he became conductor of the Tivoli Orchestra. Tivoli Gardens, developed by writer-architect Georg Carstensen and opened in August of 1843, had from its inception supported a summer orchestra. During the years when Andersen's father performed in the orchestra, Hans Christian Lumbye served as its conductor. Lumbye, well known as a dance music composer, was immensely popular with Tivoli audiences. He defined Tivoli's musical personality during his thirty-year tenure with the orchestra, and his *Champagne Galop* became the Gardens' signature composition. The light-hearted Galop enchanted nineteenth-century audiences, and even today, the champagne cork and notes of its melody decorate the balcony of the concert hall.

Lumbye's musical vision continued under conductor Balduin Dahl and subsequently under Lumbye's son, Georg. Georg led the orchestra until 1897 when he resigned his position because of illness. Violinist-conductor Franz Schnedler-Petersen (1867-1938) was selected as interim conductor with Andersen, Louis Ganne, and Emil Hartmann also conducting some of the concerts. Andersen and Schnedler-Petersen were both finalists for the permanent position, and according to Schnedler-Petersen:

The Tivoli management was inclined to appoint me, since I had done so well during the last season, and several thousand people signed a petition in my favor. Nevertheless Joachim Andersen was chosen because of his age and because of his tongue disease. And by the new year [1898], he was appointed. Thrane, the chairman of the Tivoli board, offered me the position of concertmaster on very favorable terms, but when I was told that Joachim Andersen had been furiously angry because I had dared to compete with him, I recalled my years in Berlin under an unkind conductor and refused the offer. (B70, pp. 52-53)

In hindsight, Schnedler-Petersen reflected:

Today I realize that it was good for my development that Joachim Andersen was appointed, and that I was not chosen to be the conductor because of my relatively young age. But at the time, I felt very disappointed and passed over. (B70, pp. 52-53)

(Ten years later, following Andersen's death, Schnedler-Petersen was contacted in Finland. He immediately returned to Copenhagen and became Tivoli's conductor. He also took over the Palace Concerts the following year.)

Tivoli's Board of Directors met on January 26, 1898, to grant Andersen the position of conductor. An article in the *Dannebrog* the following day reported Andersen's goals with regard to his new position, suggested public concern about the Board's choice, and revealed Andersen's defensiveness:

At Home with Joachim Andersen

Asked about his future plans for the Tivoli Orchestra, Joachim Andersen responded:

I answer with pleasure, and I am thankful for this opportunity to state publicly what I want to do as a conductor after all the rumors that have been going on about what would happen after Mr. Georg Lumbye's death. I want to follow the line of Balduin Dahl: playing new music, not turning Tivoli's concert hall into a gray musical reform school, but playing a mixture of light and serious music for which the public has shown much enthusiasm. Much has been said about me lately—nice things and wrong things—and it is the latter that I think of when I wish to assure your readers that I also highly regard a waltz by H. C. Lumbye or Strauss, and of course I shall include them in the repertoire. It is said that in my Palace Concerts I play only the most "classical"—now called "fine" music. But during the hour-and-a-half that these infrequent concerts last [Andersen's interpretation; the concerts were performed weekly], I stand before a devoted audience which expects me to present exactly what I try to give them: the greatest music.

I am going to follow this principle for my twice-weekly symphony concerts in Tivoli.

But it is far from accurate for people to say that I am not interested in light classical music which can be enjoyed together with lunch and a cigar. After all, I was among the founders of the Berlin Philharmonic Orchestra. This orchestra is now the center of Berlin's concert life and plays in a hall which serves food and drink, except on symphony evenings [the most formal concerts]. This is my plan for the winter season. It has not yet been possible in the [Odd-Fellow] Palace, but I hope it will be in the future.

Asked about the number of musicians, Joachim Andersen said: I have 45 musicians in the Palace orchestra, and in Tivoli there are 41 chairs for the daily concerts and approximately 50 for symphony evenings. All my musicians share my ideas about discipline. (B19, 28 January 1898)

During his eleven-year tenure with the orchestra, Andersen conducted a major symphony concert every Saturday night during June, July, and August, plus, on other nights of the week, three free shorter performances at 7:00, 8:30, and 10:00. He conducted a huge repertoire ranging from J. S. Bach to Richard Strauss, and gradually incorporated chamber music, choral works, and vocal solos into the Tivoli programs. Andersen always paid particular attention to Nordic composers, premiering many of their compositions. (B26, pp. 196-7)

Before Andersen, Tivoli's conductors had led the orchestra while facing the audience. But with Andersen, more challenging and serious music was added to the concert programs, requiring the conductor to face the musicians and collaborate more directly with them during performances. The change, a striking departure from the Tivoli tradition, became an amusing sidelight when cartoonists began to focus on the appearance of the back of Andersen's almost-bald head. In drawings, the conspicuous part down the back of his head extended down the back of his coat to the bottom of his coattails. The most famous cartoon by Axel Thiess, first published in the satirical weekly *Klods Hans* on February 10, 1901, showed Andersen's dachshund, Pizz, walking behind him, and the line continued as a part down the back of the dog's hair ending at its tail. Andersen, well aware of the joke, often signed correspondence with a drawing of himself showing the trademark part.

Leadership Style and Resulting Conflicts

The Tivoli Orchestra had performed rather unprofessionally during the years immediately preceding Andersen's appointment (B9), but the new conductor immediately introduced strict discipline and order. His capacity for work was enormous, and he maintained a rigorous rehearsal schedule, at times rehearsing three or four hours without a break. During these years he was celebrated as a dedicated conductor who, through tireless efforts, gave the music of Tivoli a renaissance and made it a center of Scandinavian musical life.

While Andersen's achievements were laudable, the musicians in his orchestras often resented what they perceived to be an uncompromising manner, and many controversies developed. "Especially during the early years, Joachim was almost hated and this was publicly known." (B69, p. 129) According to trombonist Anton Hansen, Andersen "suffered no opposition and fired even the most talented people without mercy for the most minor offenses... His behavior was Prussian in the worst sense of the word. No one was allowed to complain. He behaved like an absolute monarch." (B69, pp. 129 and 131)

In his memoirs, Hansen related several examples of confrontation between Andersen and the orchestra including the following:

> A couple of days ago, one of the musicians, a Mr. Skjerne [principal clarinetist] left in anger because the conductor refused to allow him ten minutes for lunch. The discontent culminated during a rehearsal when the conductor mentioned an upcoming celebration where one colleague would be honored. 'Well, gentlemen, how about the lunch tomorrow?' said the conductor. Immediately, a member of the orchestra stood up and said, 'Sorry, Maestro, I have been asked by the members of the orchestra to let you know that if you show up at the lunch tomorrow, everybody else will stay away.' One can imagine the conductor's face when he heard this. He mumbled something to the effect that he had never been subjected to such scandalous behavior. (B69, p. 129)

Hansen also detailed another incident in which

> One summer, one of the musicians very quietly agitated for a raise of one-quarter crown per evening. Joachim

became aware of this and the rebel was put on the black list. During a rehearsal, Joachim made a speech in which he emphasized that he would not tolerate any kind of socialist or anarchist behavior. In order to protect the colleague whose job was now in jeopardy, we had to reassure the boss that we would not talk further about salaries. (B69, p. 130)

The employment contract between Andersen and his musicians was strict and explicit. It clearly stated the number and length of services to be performed and the salary which would be paid. Also included in the contract was a statement declaring that the performer must "willingly and energetically support the undersigned Joachim Andersen in his efforts to achieve the best possible artistic results, and must therefore obey what the conductor or his assistant says." The final statement began:

> If this contract is not followed properly by Mr........., he shall pay 50 crowns to the musicians' union charity fund. If Mr......... refuses to begin his employment... or wishes to terminate it before the scheduled time, or if there is a serious breach of contract that Joachim Andersen feels inclined to enforce, Mr......... will pay 125 crowns to the charity fund, and will forfeit the rest of his salary. (B7)

Other regulations included a system for fining members who were late for rehearsals. The regulations concluded with the statement: "Any breach of good behavior which members commit toward the audience, conductor, assistant, or colleagues will lead to immediate dismissal from the orchestra." (B7)

One of the biggest conflicts Andersen endured involved his alleged refusal to allow members of the Palace orchestra to perform in an orchestra conducted by Franz Schnedler-Petersen, who had lost the Tivoli position to Andersen but returned intermittently to Copenhagen. The bitter dispute played itself out in a series of articles and letters in the *Politiken*, beginning on December 9, 1898, with a communication from Andersen's rival:

[Schnedler-Petersen's] Winter Concerts and [Andersen's] Palace Concerts

> Since a few of my musicians are not available to play with my orchestra Sunday nights, I have tried in vain to employ three members of Mr. Joachim Andersen's orchestra, who are the only musicians free on those evenings. All of them say they would like to fill these chairs, but that they

dare not because of Mr. Andersen's former "appeal," and because they fear losing their chairs in the Tivoli Orchestra.

Thanking the press and public for their interest, I regret to announce that I have to suspend my planned Winter Concerts because of one man's resentment of my plans. (B20, 9 December 1898)

Andersen did not respond to Schnedler-Petersen's accusation until prodded to do so by a second article two weeks later. On December 22, 1898, Andersen wrote:

Mr. Editor:

In two small articles about the Palace Concerts and the Winter Concerts on the 9th and the 20th of this month, blame has been placed on me for the suspension of the Winter Concerts.

They also state that the conductor, in no uncertain terms, has told his musicians that if they get involved in the other orchestra, they will immediately lose their seats in the Tivoli Orchestra.

Although it should seem obvious that I could never behave in this way, and that these are all rumors which lack confirmation from the musicians, I shall not allow two articles to go unanswered. Yet I shall not fatigue the readers with long-winded explanations, since they are of absolutely no value.

Unless the musicians themselves complain in public, I shall not give further details concerning the problems that may occur.

Yours,
Joachim Andersen

Mr. Joachim Andersen's statement is rather obtuse, but the essence seems to be as follows:

1). It is a vicious lie that he would tell his musicians to leave their seats if they played with Schnedler-Petersen.

2). Further explanation, which should be super-fluous, will only be given at the request of the musicians.

At this time, we think that the musicians who wish to play with Mr. Schnedler-Petersen should come forth and say what is going on and why they dare not express themselves. The *Politiken* is at the disposal of the musicians if their conductor should offend them. This, we hope, will not happen

since we wish for the sake of our concert life that the worthy
conductor Joachim Andersen will continue to be on good terms
with his musicians. (B20, 22 December 1898)

The next article, from Andersen, simply stated that readers should refer to his
article from the previous Thursday.   Two days later, Schnedler-Petersen, furious
that Andersen continued to sidestep the issue and had accused him of lying, wrote
another letter to the *Politiken* boldly stating: "Mr. Andersen's memory is
incorrect when he claims not to have expressed himself in a way that several of
his musicians and I have understood as an order." (B20, 28 December 1898)
Schnedler-Petersen again pressed Andersen to respond directly to the issue and to
state unequivocally that he would not mind if his musicians played with
Schnedler-Petersen and that it would not harm their relationship with Andersen.
But the omnipotent Andersen would not respond and would not yield.

Trouble surfaced again in 1904.   According to Anton Hansen, the one
musician for whom Andersen would make allowances was the concertmaster,
Ferdinand Hemme, whose musical ability he admired very much. (B69, pp. 129-
130) However, even Mr. Hemme was eventually fired after Andersen discovered
that he had tried to undermine the conductor's power by working to create a
union for the violinists while Andersen was in Wiesbaden.   Another series of
articles in the *Politiken*, beginning October 27, 1904, recounted the events:

The Orchestra Conflict
Long-winded Negotiations
Joachim Andersen and his Musicians

Rumors about the newly created "Violinists' Union"
and its demands for considerable salary raises for concerts and
rehearsals reached Joachim Andersen at lightning speed.   He
was away on a rest-cure, but returned six days early and began
to contact the different parties involved in the conflict.

The Palace Concerts were, of course, the main topic.
The conductor, publisher Wilhelm Hansen, Dr. Petrus Beyer,
and others met with the gentlemen of the strings in the
morning and with the gentlemen of the winds in the afternoon.

As far as we know, the conductor was by no means
willing to raise the salaries for the strings, and criticized them
for making their own union without including the winds, an
act he found disloyal toward their colleagues.

The winds expressed the same views, and this may be
the soft spot in the whole affair.

Later it was said that the winds and the strings of the

Palace orchestra would get together this evening. (B20, 27 October, 1904)

Politiken, November 4, 1904:

The Orchestra Conflict
Mr. Joachim Andersen's Statements
"The Violinists' Union"

As mentioned earlier in this paper, there have been some disagreements between members of the orchestra and its conductor. The question is money. The musicians naturally find that they earn too little for their efforts, especially for rehearsing. The demand for raises is not new to those who made the demand nor to their employers, the musical societies, nor to concert hall boards. So it should not really be a surprise to Mr. Joachim Andersen or the other orchestra leaders. The surprise, however, was that the musicians put forward their demands immediately before the beginning of the concert season. This is what has caused bitter feelings. Mr. Joachim Andersen was very angry when we spoke to him yesterday.

"I was in Wiesbaden when I received a letter from my concertmaster, Mr. Hemme, who referred to a private talk I had with him some months ago, when he advised me of the musicians' demand for increased wages. I was very understanding and said that I was willing to negotiate with the musicians, and at this time, I am still willing to address their reasonable demands. But as I continued to read his letter, I became very upset learning that twenty-five of my musicians had, in fact, formed a union, "The Violinists' Union." I would call this letter a threat.

"So, as you see, I returned immediately. I find it disloyal to me for them to form a union when I had agreed to negotiate, and I also consider them poor colleagues to create a separate union [from other musicians in the orchestra].

"Now the Violinists' Union has given up its demands, but had it not done so, I would have hired other musicians. After all, these twenty-five violinists are not the only violinists.

"But because of this mess, I had to give up the first two Palace Concerts. We will begin next Sunday. And then we will have peace, I hope.

"Who says we lack passion in this country! I hardly
set foot on Copenhagen soil before I experienced the opposite."
So much for Mr. Joachim Andersen.

"The Violinists' Union" had a meeting yesterday
morning in Larsen's Boarding House together with all of the
musicians from the orchestra. They decided to give up all
demands. But because all of the musicians participated in the
meeting, it appears to be the beginning of something.

As to the need for such a union after this, no one
knows. The conflict may be resolved. One may hope that this
occurs with less turbulence than what we have just witnessed.

Making a judgement between the two parties in this
matter would be unjust. There must still be a lot of meetings
and discussions before the questions are answered.   The
musicians have not had their last word, but toward the end of
the week, we hope to bring our readers the result of the conflict.
(Signed: Pen) (B20, 4 November 1904)

Two weeks later (November 20, 1904), the concluding article:

Orchestra Conflict
Concertmaster Hemme's Dismissal
The End

This should be the end of the orchestra conflict as the
head of the riot, concertmaster Hemme, was dismissed from
both the Tivoli and Palace orchestras.

Mr. Joachim Andersen has taken resolute action,
showing the ability of a general with energy and authority to
defeat mutiny.

His behavior in this matter will surely make the
popular conductor even more admired in the eyes of his faithful
Palace and Tivoli audiences. The gentlemen violinists led by
Mr. Hemme have not acted very wisely.

Why hide the fact that the "Violinists' Union" and its
disloyal behavior toward the conductor and colleagues neither
deserve sympathy nor have gained such.

They have been naive, and have admitted this, and
have knuckled under and agreed to play under the usual
conditions.

But Mr. Joachim Andersen could not forgive the

mastermind and dismissed him. Of course, it would have been nice if the members of the "Violinists' Union" had refused to play if Mr. Hemme did not remain concertmaster, but with financial and family issues in the picture and the loose organization of the "Union," the musicians did not dare to take such a step. (B20, 20 November 1904)

Conducting Technique

Andersen's primary conducting model was Hans von Bülow, under whom he had performed while in Berlin. Sources agree that Andersen was not a great conductor, but that he was a refined, cosmopolitan man who looked elegant in front of the orchestra. (B26, p. 196) Numerous anecdotes concerning his flawed conducting technique include this account:

> His beat was not blameless and not too clear, nor were his eager signals to the principal winds and hectic waving and cueing to the different groups of instruments. All this confirmed that the muses had not endowed him with the gift of making clear the silent language of the baton. (Gandrup, B7)

Julius Clausen, in his book *Mennesker paa min vej*, related: "when attempting a completely new undertaking, he would make strange mistakes in tempo." (B60, p. 180) And Anton Hansen colorfully described his impression of Andersen's conducting:

> All Joachim Andersen's performances and especially the symphonies were carefully rehearsed and he never relaxed. At times, and especially when he was nervous, his beat would become vague, though still energetic, and as a result the orchestra at times would falter. If he became aware that the sinking ship could not be righted again, he would stop and start all over. During such mishaps, he would behave like a crazy man, and if he couldn't vent his anger at anybody else, he would kick his little dachshund, "Pizz," if he were unlucky enough to be close by. Of course that didn't help any more than did his vague statements about sabotage and carelessness. These scenes were frustrating, especially for those of us who wanted to do our best. And if anybody had had the audacity to tell him the real reason for the calamity—his own unintelligible beat—then that person would probably have been fired on the spot. (B69, p. 130)

Still, in spite of these flaws, Andersen was remembered after his death as a man who "through enormous skill and effort worked to refine musical taste in the environs in which he worked." (B20, 8 May 1909)   The *Orkesterforeningens Medlemsblad* (the musicians' union paper) published an obituary in June of 1909 stating:

> With this death, the orchestra society and the music profession as a whole have lost a very advanced personality. Few have made such an impression on Danish musical life as he. His efforts in this area have been significant. He wanted to educate and wanted to improve people's taste for wholesome and good music. And Joachim Andersen had the ability to do just that. He understood how to make the most of this ability through tireless and conscientious work. We musicians can only be grateful for each of his contributions in his attempt to improve music. Joachim Andersen's fourteen years of work here in Copenhagen have yielded great benefits.
> He has raised the profession's standard. As already expressed at the society's recently held meeting, Joachim Andersen had his sharp edges. He could be tough when it involved advancing the musical goal. That in this he collided with some of his musicians is understandable. But he also proved that he was fond of the musicians and he probably wished nothing more than to achieve the highest possible artistic result and to be respected by his musicians. (B62, p. 82)

Final Years

On February 6, 1898, the new Historic Collection of Musical Instruments in Copenhagen (now renamed the Music History Museum and Carl Claudius Collection) sponsored a concert featuring performers playing instruments from the collection. Joachim Andersen and Golla Hammerich opened the program with a performance of two movements from flute sonatas of Frederick the Great of Prussia. Andersen played a one-keyed flute donated by Danish poet Jens Baggesen (1764-1826); Hammerich played a clavier previously owned by Danish composer C. E. F. Weyse. This is the only known flute performance given by Andersen following his return to Copenhagen.

The city of Copenhagen inaugurated a new series of free summer concerts in 1899. Andersen was chosen to be the conductor of these concerts to be presented in the Rosenborg Gardens. However, because the Tivoli Board of Directors would not amend his contract which forbade conducting elsewhere during the Tivoli season, Andersen rehearsed the programs and Ferdinand Hemme conducted the performances until Andersen was able to take over some years later.

During the final years of his life, Andersen wrote a little-known and never-published pedagogical treatise on counterpoint (1901) which is now housed at the Danish Royal Library. In 1905 he was knighted and, on March 1st of the same year, the Ministry of War appointed him a member of the board which examined Danish military bands. Andersen received the title of Professor shortly before his death.

Just before the end of the 1908-09 season, Joachim Andersen resigned as conductor of the Palace Concerts because of illness. His final concert with the orchestra took place on the 28th of March. There was to have been one more concert that season, but it did not occur. Following the March 28th concert, "the exhausted conductor called his orchestra together to say good-bye, and fell into tears while trying to tell them that he had to retire." (Gandrup, B7) According to a writer for the *Orkesterforeningens Medlemsblad*, Andersen, "with a very emotional and eventually failing voice, thanked his musicians for their cooperation and good work. He made a gripping impression on each of them." (B62, p. 83)

A short time later, Andersen was admitted to the Hareskov Sanatorium where he hoped to rest and gain strength for the upcoming Tivoli season. Instead, his health declined and on May 7, 1909 (one week before the opening of the Tivoli season), he died at the age of sixty-two. Doctor S. Hytten provided an account of the final days of his friend's life:

> ...He seemed well until the left side of his body became lame on Thursday night. He got better over the next day, and could speak and move his leg. Over night, he got worse, the attacks continued, and he was unconscious until today. I did not expect a catastrophe and was talking with Joachim Andersen's wife on the veranda when I was called to his bedside. I realized that death was calling, and my good friend died quietly and peacefully. At 4:30 he expired. His wife then came to his side. (B19, 9 August 1909)

Victor Gandrup, who compiled notes for a biography which he did not complete, attempted to solve the mystery of the cause of Andersen's death, and notes of his findings are now housed at the Music History Museum in Copenhagen. By contacting colleagues and doctors who had known Andersen, he tried to ascertain whether there had been any degeneration in Andersen's health during the last years of his life. The duration of degeneration would help to determine the cause of death. His research revealed that Andersen had experienced blindness in one eye during the last years of his life, had apologized to his orchestra for sitting down while conducting, and had, according to Thorvold Nielsen, suffered a "rapid failing of health" during his final year of work with the Orchestra School. (Gandrup, B7) These afflictions suggest the gradual decline of health generally associated with syphilis as opposed to the rapid degeneration associated with a stroke, though the latter was cited as the cause of death on the death certificate.

While it is generally believed that he died at the Hareskov Sanatorium, a letter to Dr. Arne Portman (writer unknown) stated:

> There exists no file on Joachim Andersen. It seems to have disappeared. It was written in a book kept by Axel Hansen which is in the possession of the Nissen family. I do not think he died in the sanatorium, as a doctor from the outside wrote the death certificate. (Gandrup, B7)

The letter continued:

> I'll try to find the book, but do not expect too much, as death certificates do not inform of unmentionable diseases, from which he might well have suffered. (Gandrup, B7)

After Andersen's death, his urn was placed in a columbary. During subsequent years, Louis Wolf, a wealthy Danish merchant, paid all of the expenses to have the urn maintained at Bispebjerg cemetery. Years later, however, when he went to place a flower on the urn, Wolf found that it was no longer in the columbary. By some mistake the urn had been buried in a common grave. A letter from Mr. Rasmussen of the Kobenhavns Begravelsesvæsens Konter (the grave registry) explained:

> In reply to your question of the 2nd of this month, I can tell you that the ashes of Carl Joachim Andersen were moved from the columbary to the cemetery's storeroom on January 20, 1942, and on January 9, 1943, were buried in Bispebjerg cemetery. (Gandrup, B7)

Wolf was, of course, furious. After paying the expenses for more than thirty years, he learned that Andersen's ashes had been placed in a common grave, and no one had ever informed him of the change.

Andersen's ashes remain in the large Bispebjerg cemetery at the northwest end of Copenhagen, although there is still no marker to identify the place where the urn is buried. His flute and some personal belongings were given to Robert Enevoldsen, a former student and member of Andersen's professional orchestras in Copenhagen. Enevoldsen sold the flute to Tivoli Gardens in 1934 or 1935; the instrument probably burned in June of 1944 when Tivoli and most of its archives were destroyed during the German occupation of Denmark in World War II. A bust of Andersen which was created by Sophie Claudius and displayed at Tivoli was also destroyed during that tumultuous time.

Just as the mortal remains of the virtuoso flutist, composer, and conductor are relegated to an obscure grave, much of his life and work lingers in mystery—manuscripts of his compositions burned, school records lost, medical records discarded, his eight-keyed wooden flute destroyed. Only sketchily accounted for are his years in St. Petersburg and those before his return to Copenhagen. Even Andersen in his personally written *curriculum vitae* omits mention of these long periods in his life.

He began his career in the poorest section of Copenhagen, rose to prominence in Denmark and later in Berlin, where he became the colleague and friend of the greatest musicians of the late nineteenth century. Then, suddenly, in the midst of glorious years performing under Hans von Bülow and conducting the Berlin Philharmonic Orchestra, his career ended abruptly, his brother, mother, father, and son died in rapid succession, and he suffered the tragic effects of syphilis as he struggled to build a new musical career in Copenhagen. He alienated musicians in his orchestras with his autocratic approach, but he persevered, never allowing obstructions to divert him from his unwavering path, until he was overcome by illness and exhaustion.

Andersen's steadfast devotion to music guided his life and contributed to the founding of one of the world's greatest orchestras, the expansion of cultural opportunities in Copenhagen, and most notably, the composition of 186 etudes which have challenged and inspired every serious flutist for a century. These pieces are Joachim Andersen's legacy, they inform us of his virtuosity as a performer and his sensitivity as a composer, and they remain a powerful measure of excellence for flutists around the world.

Catalogue of Compositions

All known compositions by Joachim Andersen are detailed in this Catalogue of Compositions. Material has been compiled directly from Andersen's first-edition scores at the New York Public Library (B2) and, secondarily, from scores at the Danish Royal Library in Copenhagen. (B1) Particularly valuable has been the collection of programs and related materials compiled between 1890 and 1909 by Andersen's second wife and donated to the New York Public Library in 1912 and 1913. (B9) Additional resources include programs reviewed at the National Institute for Music Research in Berlin (B10), original publication contracts retained by the Wilhelm Hansen Publishing Company in Copenhagen (B14), repertoire catalogues, and contemporary Danish newspapers (B17, B19, B20) researched on-site in Copenhagen. Manuscript information not included is believed to have been lost in a fire at the Berlin Philharmonic Orchestra's summer home in Scheveningen, Holland, in 1896.

While it is difficult to determine precisely when Andersen wrote his compositions, first-edition publication information suggests that the early opus numbers were written during his years in St. Petersburg and first years in Berlin, op. 24, 33, 35, 37, and most of the surrounding opus numbers were written during his later years in Berlin, and the final opus numbers (op. 57 through 63), the piano compositions, and the three transcriptions without opus numbers (W52, W53, and W54), were composed after his return to Copenhagen. Intriguing associations may be inferred from the often poignant dedications Andersen made to his family, friends, and colleagues, as well as from his handwritten messages to individuals on first-edition scores. To facilitate these correlations, the Catalogue, where possible, includes identification of these individuals as well as references to page numbers in the Biography where they are mentioned.

Publication information changes frequently, but a section "Subsequent Editions" is included to give the reader a sense of the acceptance and popularity of Andersen's compositions. The opus 33 collection of etudes, for example, has been published by no fewer than ten companies in recent years, while the Tarantella, op. 10, has never been republished since Max Leichssenring's edition. The Wilhelm Hansen Publishing Company in Copenhagen has recently begun printing photocopies of previously out-of-print first editions.   These photocopies as well as recent editions by other publishers indicate renewed interest in Andersen's flute and piano works.

Compositions with Opus Numbers

W1

Op. 2   **UNGARISCHE FANTASIE** [a minor → A major]
(flute with piano or orchestral accompaniment)

> First edition: Hamburg, Max Leichssenring, n.d. (Plate no. 229)
> Andersen's copy is housed at the New York Public Library (vol. 2 of complete works); Danish Royal Library houses a second first-edition copy.

> Subsequent editions: Rühle & Wendling, Cundy-Bettoney in *Pleasures of Pan*, vol. 5
> (No longer in print)

> Dedication: "Herrn Heinrich Gantenberg, Kgl. Kammermusiker und Lehrer an der Kgl. Hochschule für ausübende Tonkunst zu Berlin hochachtungsvoll gewidmet"
> [Respectfully dedicated to Mr. Heinrich Gantenberg, Royal chamber musician and teacher at the Royal Academy of Music in Berlin]

> Additional information: Danish Royal Library catalogue card provides orchestral instrumentation: "Stemmer 22 bd.: 4 vl I, 3 vl II, 2 vla, 2 vlc, 2 cb, fl I+II: fl piccolo, ob I+II, cl I/II + fag II, fag I, cor I+II, tr I+II, trb, timp 2"

W2

Op. 3   **CONCERTSTÜCK** [E major]
(flute with piano or orchestral accompaniment)

> First edition: Hamburg, Max Leichssenring, n.d. (Plate no. 168)
> Andersen's copy is housed at the New York Public Library (vol. 2 of complete works); Danish Royal Library houses a second first-edition copy.

Subsequent editions: Rühle & Wendling
   (No longer in print)

Dedication: "Seinem Freunde Herrn Wilhelm Tieftrunk gewidmet"
   [Dedicated to his friend Mr. Wilhelm Tieftrunk]
   (Wilhelm Tieftrunk was principal flutist of the Hamburg
   Symphony Orchestra.) See Biography, pp. 7-8.

Selected performances: Emil Prill (student of Joachim Andersen and,
   beginning in 1891, principal flutist of the Berlin Royal Opera)
   with the Tivoli Orchestra, conducted by Joachim Andersen, August
   26, 1901. See Biography, pp. 9-10.

Approximate date of composition: In a personal letter from Paul
   Taffanel to Joachim Andersen, dated May 5, 1895, Taffanel referred
   to op. 3, writing: It "would be a true joy for me to cause to be
   played a new work of yours in this same hall where I performed
   your beautiful *Concertstück* twelve years ago." (B8)

Additional information: Danish Royal Library catalogue card provides
   orchestral instrumentation: "Stemmer 30 bd.: 4 vl I/II, 3 vla, 3
   vlc, 3 cb, fl, ob I/II, cl I/II, fag I/II, cor I/II, tr I/II, trb, timp 2"
   This composition was selected as the examination piece for the
   Paris Conservatory's *concours* in 1895.

W 3

Op. 5   **BALLADE ET DANSE DES SYLPHES** [a minor]
   (flute with piano or orchestral accompaniment)

First edition: Paris, Brandus & Cie, n.d. (Plate no. 895)
   Andersen's copy is housed at the New York Public Library (vol. 2
   of complete works); Danish Royal Library houses a second first-
   edition copy.

Subsequent editions: Billaudot, Joubert, Maquet, Southern

Dedication: "A Monsieur le Baron de Korff"
   (Written in pencil on Andersen's copy: "Meyerbeer's son-in-law")

Additional information: Paul Taffanel mentioned this piece in a letter
   to Joachim Andersen, dated July 1883. (B8)
   Duration: 10 minutes, 50 seconds

W4

Op. 6   **DEUX MORCEAUX DE SALON**
#1 Solitude (Einsamkeit) [e minor → E major]
#2 Désir (Wunsch) [a minor → C major]
(flute with piano accompaniment)

First edition: Hamburg, Max Leichssenring, n.d. (Plate no. 329)
Andersen's copy is housed at the New York Public Library (vol. 4
of complete works); Danish Royal Library houses a second first-
edition copy.

Subsequent editions: Rühle & Wendling
(No longer in print)

Dedication: "à Fräulein Bertha Lechler verehrungsvoll gewidmet"
[Dedicated with respect to Miss Bertha Lechler]

W5

Op. 7   **IMPROMPTU** [C major]
(flute with piano accompaniment)

First edition: Hamburg, Max Leichssenring, n.d. (Plate no. 330)
Andersen's copy is housed at the New York Public Library (vol. 4
of complete works); Danish Royal Library houses a second first-
edition copy.

Subsequent editions: Rühle & Wendling, European American Music
Corp. in *The Andersen Collection*

Dedication: "à Monsieur Paul Taffanel"
(Paul Taffanel was Professor of Flute at the Paris Conservatory
between 1893 and 1908.) See Biography, pp. 11-12 and 14.

W6

Op. 8   **MOTO PERPETUO** [e minor]
(flute with piano or orchestral accompaniment)

First edition: Hamburg, Max Leichssenring, n.d. (Plate no. 331)
Andersen's copy is housed at the New York Public Library (vol. 2
of complete works); Danish Royal Library houses a second first-
edition copy.

Subsequent editions: Rühle & Wendling, Billaudot, Zimmermann

Dedication: "A Monsieur Paul Taffanel"
   (Paul Taffanel was Professor of Flute at the Paris Conservatory
   between 1893 and 1908.) See Biography, pp. 11-12 and 14.

Additional information: Cues for orchestral instruments are handwritten
   into the piano score of Andersen's copy; Metronome marking is
   changed from 152 to 160 in Andersen's copy.

W7

Op. 9   **AU BORD DE LA MER, MORCEAU DE SALON**
[a minor]
(flute with piano accompaniment)

First edition: Hamburg, Max Leichssenring, n.d. (Plate no. 371)
   Andersen's copy is housed at the New York Public Library (vol. 4
   of complete works); Danish Royal Library houses a second first-
   edition copy.

Subsequent editions: Rühle & Wendling, Oxford University Press in
   Five Songs Without Words

Dedication: "A Monsieur le Professeur Moritz Fürstenau Chevalier de
   plusieurs Ordres"
   [To Professor Moritz Fürstenau, Knight of Several Orders]
   (Moritz Fürstenau was a flutist with the Dresden Symphony Orchestra and Professor at the Dresden Conservatory between 1858 and
   1889.)

W8

Op. 10   **TARANTELLA** [b minor]
(flute with piano or orchestral accompaniment)

First edition: Hamburg, Max Leichssenring, n.d. (Plate no. 372)
   Andersen's copy is housed at the New York Public Library (vol. 4
   of complete works); Danish Royal Library houses a second first-
   edition copy.

Subsequent editions: None
   (No longer in print)

Dedication: "Herrn Wilhelm Barge, Lehrer am Conservatorium der
Musik zu Leipzig hochachtungsvoll gewidmet"
[Respectfully dedicated to Mr. Wilhelm Barge, teacher at the Music
Conservatory in Leipzig]

W9
Op. 15 **24 GROSSE ETUDEN** [All major and minor keys]
(flute alone)

First edition: Hamburg, Max Leichssenring, n.d. (Plate no. 421)
Andersen's copy is housed at the New York Public Library (vol. 1
of complete works); Danish Royal Library houses the Rühle &
Wendling edition.

Subsequent editions: Bèrben, Billaudot, Edu-tainment, Carl Fischer,
International, Novello, Schirmer, Southern

Dedication: "Meinem lieben Vater und Lehrer, C. J. Andersen"
[To my beloved father and teacher, C. J. Andersen]
See Biography, pp. 1-2.

W10
Op. 16 **FANTAISIE CARACTÉRISTIQUE** [a minor→ A major]
(flute with piano or orchestral accompaniment)

First edition: Hamburg, August Cranz, n.d. (Plate no. AC36770)
Andersen's copy is housed at the New York Public Library (vol. 2
of complete works).

Subsequent editions: None
(No longer in print)

Dedication: "à son frère, Vigo Andersen, Membre de l'Orchestre royale
à Copenhague"
[to his brother, Vigo Andersen, Member of the Royal Orchestra of
Copenhagen] See Biography, pp. 3 and 18-19.

Selected performances: Ary van Leeuwen (student of Joachim Andersen
and principal flutist of the Vienna Opera) with the Tivoli Orchestra,
conducted by Joachim Andersen, July 5, 1905. This was the
piece's first performance in Tivoli Concert Hall. See Biography,
p. 9; Performed in Tivoli Concert Hall a second time (after
Andersen's death) in July of 1911.

Approximate date of composition: between 1878 and 1885 (These dates
correspond in part with the dates that Vigo Andersen was employed
as flutist with the Royal Orchestra in Copenhagen.)

Additional information: Andersen's copy is decoratively inscribed by
him: "Meinem lieben Freunde Wilhelm Tieftrunk, zur Frdl.
Erinnerung an Joachim Andersen Berlin: 5 Juni 1885."
[To my beloved friend Wilhelm Tieftrunk, with the hope of your
fond memories of Joachim Andersen, Berlin: June 5, 1885.]
(Wilhelm Tieftrunk was principal flutist of the Hamburg Symphony
Orchestra.) See Biography, pp. 7-8.

W11

Op. 19 **ALBUMBLATT** [A major]
(flute with piano accompaniment)

First edition: Leipzig, Robert Forsberg, n.d. (Plate no. 3515)
Andersen's copy is housed at the New York Public Library (vol. 4
of complete works); Danish Royal Library houses a second first-
edition copy.

Subsequent editions: None
(No longer in print)

Dedication: "Fräulein Mannie and Maggie Collins freundschaftlichst
gewidmet"
[Dedicated with warmest friendship to Misses Mannie and Maggie
Collins]

W12

Op. 21 **STUDIEN IN DUR UND MOLL** [All major and minor keys]
(flute alone)

First edition: Hamburg, August Cranz, 1885 (Plate no. 36842)
Andersen's copy is housed at the New York Public Library (vol. 1
of complete works); Danish Royal Library houses a second first-
edition copy.

Subsequent editions: Billaudot, International, McGinnis & Marx,
Schirmer, Southern

Dedication: "Herrn F. Waterstraat, Prof. am kaiserlich russischen Conservatory Musik St. Petersburg"
[Mr. F. Waterstraat, Professor at the Imperial Russian Conservatory of Music in St. Petersburg]

Additional information: John Fonville's document, *A Pedagogical Approach to the Flute Etudes of Joachim Andersen* (B23) provides date of 1885.

W13

Op. 22 **LA RÉSIGNATION** (MÉDITATION) [F major] **ET POLONAISE** [a minor]
(flute with piano accompaniment)

First edition: London, Rudall, Carte and Co., n.d. (Plate no. not provided)
Andersen's copy is housed at the New York Public Library (vol. 4 of complete works); Danish Royal Library houses a second first-edition copy.

Subsequent editions: None
(No longer in print)

Dedication: "à Monsieur François Hagen"

Selected performances: "La Résignation" was performed by Joachim Andersen with the Berlin Philharmonic Orchestra, conducted by Gustav Kogel, August 6, 1891. (Andersen performed this work paired with the "Babillard" of op. 24.)

Additional information: Handwritten into Andersen's copy five measures before the end of the piece is "poco string. ------"; line lasts two measures, at which point there is a "rall." marked. (B2)

W14

Op. 23 **GAVOTTE** [D major]
(flute with piano accompaniment)

First edition: London, Rudall, Carte and Co., n.d. (Plate no. not provided)
Andersen's copy is housed at the New York Public Library (vol. 4 of complete works).

Subsequent editions: None
  (No longer in print)

Dedication: None

W15

Op. 24   **SIX MORCEAUX DE SALON EN DEUX SUITES**
  Suite No. 1
  #1 Chant Pastorale [G major]
  #2 Rêverie [F major]
  #3 Alla Mazurka [a minor]
  Suite No. 2
  #4 Barcarolle [f minor]
  #5 Berceuse [D major]
  #6 Babillard [G major]
  (flute with piano accompaniment)

  First edition: Rudall, Carte & Co., n.d. (Plate no. not provided)
    Andersen's copy is housed at the New York Public Library (vol. 4
    of complete works).

  Subsequent editions: Little Piper, European American Music Corp. in
    The Andersen Collection; "Rêverie" and "Berceuse" published by
    Oxford University Press in *Five Songs Without Words*; "Berceuse"
    published by Boosey & Hawkes in *First Repertoire Pieces For
    Flute*, Novello in *A Very Easy Romantic Album for Flute and
    Piano*

  Dedication: "Dedicated to Miss Sarah Dana Watson"
    (Miss Watson became Andersen's second wife on June 2, 1891.)
    See Biography, p. 10.

  Selected performances: "Babillard" was performed by Joachim Andersen
    with the Berlin Philharmonic Orchestra, conducted by Gustav
    Kogel, August 6, 1891, August 18, 1891, and August 25, 1891.
    (On August 6, 1891, Andersen performed the work paired with the
    "Résignation" of op. 22; On August 18, 1891, and August 25,
    1891, Andersen performed the work paired with the "Andante" by
    Molique.) The "Babillard" was also performed by Johannes
    Ahlquist (student of Joachim Andersen) at an Orchestra School
    concert at the Odd-Fellow Palace, conducted by Joachim Andersen,
    May 8, 1904. (Ahlquist performed this work paired with the
    "Legende" of op. 55.) See Biography, p. 21.

W16

Op. 26 **VARIATIONS DROLATIQUES SUR UN AIR SUÉDOIS**
[G major]
(flute with piano or orchestral accompaniment)

First edition: Hamburg, Max Leichssenring, n.d. (Plate no. 605)
Andersen's copy is housed at the New York Public Library (vol. 2
of complete works); Danish Royal Library houses a second first-
edition copy.

Subsequent editions: Billaudot, Cundy-Bettoney, Carl Fischer

Dedication: "A Wilhelm Popp"
(Wilhelm Popp was principal flutist of the Hamburg Philharmonic
Orchestra.)

Selected performances: Joachim Andersen, with the Berlin Philharmonic
Orchestra, conducted by Gustav Kogel, March 8, 1891; Emil Prill
(student of Joachim Andersen and, beginning in 1891, principal flutist of the Berlin Royal Opera) with the Tivoli Orchestra, conducted
by Joachim Andersen, August 27, 1901. See Biography, pp. 9-10.

Additional information: Danish Royal Library catalogue card provides
orchestral instrumentation: "Stemmer 22 bd.: 3 vl I/II, 3 vla, 2
vlc, 2 cb, fl I+II, ob I+II, cl I+II, fag I+II, cor I/II, tr I + perc, tr II
+ timp, clochettes Overskriftstitel. 2"
Orchestral instrument cues are written into the piano score of the
Danish Royal Library copy.

W17

Op. 27 **VARIATIONS ELÉGIAQUES** [d minor]
(flute with piano accompaniment)

First edition: Hamburg, Max Leichssenring, n.d. (Plate no. 606)
Andersen's copy is housed at the New York Public Library (vol. 2
of complete works); Danish Royal Library houses a second first-
edition copy.

Subsequent editions: Rühle & Wendling, Billaudot, Cundy-Bettoney,
Carl Fischer

Dedication: "A Madame Cornelie Hagen"

W18

Op. 28 **DEUX MORCEAUX**
#1 Berceuse [e minor]
(Plate no. 617)
#2 Gavotte [F major]
(Plate no. 618)
(flute with piano or orchestral accompaniment)

First edition: Hamburg, Max Leichssenring, n.d.
Andersen's copy is housed at the New York Public Library (vol. 4 of complete works); Danish Royal Library houses a second first-edition copy.

Subsequent editions: Rühle & Wendling, Billaudot, Cundy-Bettoney, Southern in *Romantic Music for Flute and Piano*, Book 2; "Berceuse" published by Oxford University Press in *Five Songs Without Words*, Novello in *A Very Easy Romantic Album for Flute and Piano*; "Berceuse" arranged for flute orchestra (four flutes, alto flute, bass flute, and bass), published by Megido Music Publications.

Dedication: "à Mademoiselle Agnes Stolzmann"

Selected performances: Joachim Andersen at a concert of soloists of the Berlin Philharmonic Orchestra, November 23, 1890.

Additional information: The piano score of Andersen's copy includes several fingering markings in pencil added for the pianist; The "Berceuse" includes some "X"s, 2 trills ‖ key change to one flat labeled "ohne ped," with a fermata at the tempo marking just after. (B2)

W19

Op. 30 **24 INSTRUKTIVE UEBUNGEN** [All major and minor keys] (flute alone)

First edition: Hamburg, Max Leichssenring, n.d. (Plate no. 619)
Andersen's copy is housed at the New York Public Library (vol. 1 of complete works); Danish Royal Library houses a second first-edition copy.

Subsequent editions: Rühle & Wendling, Bèrben, Billaudot, Edu-
tainment, International, McGinnis & Marx, Southern, Zerboni;
Three etudes (No. 12, 15, and 23) published by Ricordi in *Tre
Esercizi Istruttivi.*

Dedication: "Herrn Roman Kukula. Mitglied der K. K. Hof-Kapelle
und Hofoper. Professor am Conservatorium in Wien."
[Mr. Roman Kukula. Member of the Imperial and Royal Orchestra
and Opera. Professor at the Conservatory in Vienna.]

Additional information: Metronome markings are included in Joachim
Andersen's copy.

W20

Op. 33   **KLEINE EXERZITIEN** [All major and minor keys]
(flute alone)

First edition: Berlin, Friedrich Luckhardt, 1888
Andersen's copy is housed at the New York Public Library (vol. 1
of complete works).

Subsequent editions: Bèrben, Billaudot, Chester, Edu-tainment, Carl
Fischer, Wilhelm Hansen, International, Little Piper, Schirmer,
Southern; No. 14, 15, and 20, arranged for flute and piano by
Antonio Lora, published by Carl Fischer as *Three Humorous
Pieces*

Dedication: "Jac de Jong - (Amsterdam) Flute Solo de S. M. le Roi
des Pays-Bas, Chevalier de l'Ordre de la Couronne de Chêne"
[To Jacques de Jong (Amsterdam), solo flutist to His Majesty,
King of The Netherlands, Knight of the Order of the Oak Crown]

Additional information: Metronome markings are included in Joachim
Andersen's copy.

W21

Op. 35   **WIEN NEERLANDS BLOED FANTAISIE ÜBER   DIE
HOLLÄNDISCHE VOLKSHYMNE** [G major]
(flute with piano or orchestral accompaniment)

First edition: Hamburg, Max Leichssenring, n.d. (Plate no. 693)
Andersen's copy is housed at the New York Public Library (vol. 2
of complete works); Danish Royal Library houses a second first-
edition copy.

Subsequent editions: Rühle & Wendling
(No longer in print)

Dedication: "Herrn M. A. Reiss Generaldircctor des Seebad
Scheveningen in Verehrung gewidmet"
[Dedicated with respect to Mr. M. A. Reiss, Executive Director of
the Resort of Scheveningen]

Selected performances: Joachim Andersen with the Berlin Philharmonic
Orchestra, conducted by Gustav Kogel, December 26, 1888, July
17, 1890, January 4, 1891, March 29, 1891, and August 31, 1891;
Franz Schmeling with the Berlin Philharmonic Orchestra, conducted by Rudolf Herfurth, March 20, 1892, and July 5, 1892;
Vigo Andersen (Joachim's younger brother) performed *Fantasia for
Flute on the Dutch National Hymn* with the Chicago Orchestra,
conducted by Theodore Thomas, February 10 and 11, 1893. See
Biography, pp. 18-19. Joachim Andersen performed the *Hommage
aux Hollandais für Flöte* with the Berlin Philharmonic Orchestra,
conducted by Gustav Kogel, October 7, 1888, and again with no
date listed on the program.

Additional information: Danish Royal Library catalogue card provides
orchestral instrumentation: "Stemmer 20 bd.: 3 vl I/II, 2 vla, 2
vlc, 2cb, fl I+II, ob I+II, cl I+II, fag I+II, cor I+II, tr I+II, trb I+II,
trb III+timp 2"
Orchestral instrument cues are written into Andersen's piano score.

W22
Op. 37 **KLEINE CAPRICEN** [All major and minor keys]
(flute alone)

First edition: Copenhagen, Wilhelm Hansen, n.d.
Andersen's copy is housed at the New York Public Library (vol. 1
of complete works); Danish Royal Library houses a second first-
edition copy.

Publication contract: Signed with the Wilhelm Hansen Publishing
Company, Berlin, May 24, 1889 (B14)
(125 crowns for this collection)

Subsequent editions: Billaudot, International, McGinnis and Marx, Schirmer, Southern, #16-20 by Universal in *100 Classical Studies for Flute*, #1, 2, 4, 5, 6, 8, 10-12, 14, 18, 21, 23, 25, and 26 by Schott in *Prélude - Cadence - Capriccio, 223 Solostücke und Übungen in allen Tonarten*

Dedication: "Herrn J. Dumon, Professor am Conservatorium der Musik in Brüssel verehrungsvoll zugeeignet"
[Dedicated with respect to Mr. J. Dumon, Professor at the Conservatory of Music in Brussels]

Additional information: Metronome markings are included in Joachim Andersen's copy.

W23

Op. 41 **KLEINE STUDIEN** [Major and minor keys through four sharps and four flats]
(flute alone)

First edition: Hamburg, Max Leichssenring, n.d.
Andersen's copy (Rich Rühles edition) is housed at the New York Public Library (vol. 1 of complete works); Danish Royal Library houses a copy of the Max Leichssenring edition.

Subsequent editions: Rühle & Wendling, Billaudot, Edu-tainment, International, McGinnis & Marx, Schirmer, Southern

Dedication: "Herrn Ray Thompson freundschaftlichst zugeeignet"
[Dedicated in warmest friendship to Mr. Ray Thompson]

Additional information: Danish Royal Library catalogue card lists date of 1892 for the Max Leichssenring edition.
Metronome markings are not included in Joachim Andersen's copy.

W24

Op. 44 **L'HIRONDELLE** (VALSE CAPRICE) [D major]
(flute with piano accompaniment)

First edition: Copenhagen, Wilhelm Hansen, n.d. (Plate no. 11959)
Andersen's copy is housed at the New York Public Library (vol. 2 of complete works); Danish Royal Library houses a second first-edition copy.

Publication contract: Signed with the Wilhelm Hansen Publishing
    Company, Copenhagen, May 16, 1907 (B14)
    (1000 crowns for this piece and six others)

Subsequent editions: None
    (No longer in print)

Dedication: "A Madame Ella Françella"

W25

Op. 45 **OPERN-TRANSCRIPTIONEN**
    #1 Die Hochzeit des Figaro [Mozart] [G major]
    (Plate no. 11613)
    #2 Norma [Bellini] [E^b major]
    (Plate no. 11616)
    #3 Die Weisse Dame [Boieldieu] [D major]
    (Plate no. 11618)
    #4 Die Lustigen Weiber von Windsor [Nicolai] [G major]
    (Plate no. 11614)
    #5 Don Juan [Mozart] [a minor › A major]
    (Plate no. 11615)
    #6 Lucia di Lammermoor [Donizetti] [D major]
    (Plate no. 11617)
    #7 Der Freischütz [Weber] [C major]
    (Plate no. 11619)
    #8 Die Zauberflöte [Mozart] [D major]
    (Plate no. 11620)
    (Transcriptions for flute with piano accompaniment)

First edition: Copenhagen and Leipzig, Wilhelm Hansen, n.d.
    Andersen's copy is housed at the New York Public Library (vol. 3
    of complete works); Danish Royal Library houses a second first-
    edition copy of #1, 3, 4, 5, and 7.

Publication contract: Signed with the Wilhelm Hansen Publishing Com-
    pany, Berlin, June 12, 1894 (Six of the transcriptions were listed
    on the contract, excluding *Norma* and *Lucia di Lammermoor*.) (B14)
    (180 crowns for this piece)

Subsequent editions: *Fantasy on Bellini's "Norma"* published by
    Wilhelm Hansen in *Tango Fantasia and other short pieces from
    Denmark. Die Zauberflöte* published by Zimmermann.
    (The other transcriptions in this collection are no longer in print.)

Dedication: None

Additional information: An announcement in the *Politiken* of July 22, 1895 (B20), stated that Andersen's works would be increased with the addition of five new opus numbers during the year. The list included eight opera fantasies. A second announcement in the *Dannebrog* of March 6, 1896 (B19), stated that the pieces had recently been published and that they were fairly easy pieces which were "good for pleasing friends and family."

W26
Op. 46   WIEDERSEHEN
LIED OHNE WORTE [A major]
(flute with piano accompaniment)

First edition: Leipzig, Jules Heinrich Zimmermann, 1894 (Plate no. Z2122)
Andersen's copy is housed at the New York Public Library (vol. 4 of complete works); Danish Royal Library houses a second first-edition copy.

Subsequent editions: Albert Kunzelmann

Dedication: "Herrn und Frau J. V. B. Bleecker jr. gewidmet"
[Dedicated to Mr. and Mrs. J. V. B. Bleecker, Jr.]

W27
Op. 47   SOLOVORTRAG FÜR JUNGE FLÖTENSPIELER
THEMA MIT VARIATIONEN [G major]
(flute with piano accompaniment)

First edition: Leipzig, Jules Heinrich Zimmermann, 1894 (Plate no. Z2123)
Andersen's copy is housed at the New York Public Library (vol. 4 of complete works); Danish Royal Library houses a second first-edition copy.

Subsequent editions: None
(No longer in print)

Dedication: "Herrn Felix Sechel gewidmet"
[Dedicated to Mr. Felix Sechel]

W28

Op. 48 **ALLEGRO MILITAIRE** [E major]
(two flutes with piano or orchestral accompaniment)

First edition: Leipzig, Jules Heinrich Zimmermann, 1894 (Plate no.
Z2094)
Andersen's copy is housed at the New York Public Library (vol. 2
of complete works); Danish Royal Library houses a second first-
edition copy.

Subsequent editions: Billaudot, Southern

Dedication: "Herrn Heinrich Erichson gewidmet"
[Dedicated to Mr. Heinrich Erichson]
(Heinrich Erichson was second flutist of the Berlin Philharmonic
Orchestra during Andersen's tenure as principal flutist.)

Selected performances: Joachim Andersen and Franz Schmeling with
the Berlin Philharmonic Orchestra, conducted by Gustav Kogel,
July 6, 1890, and October 19, 1890; Leo Lottenburger and Robert
Enevoldsen with the Tivoli Orchestra, conducted by Joachim
Andersen, May 23, 1900, May 26, 1900, July 22, 1900, Septem-
ber 1, 1900, August 8, 1902, and with the Palace orchestra, con-
ducted by Joachim Andersen, December 26, 1901; Robert Enevoldsen
and Christian Agerup with the Tivoli Orchestra, conducted by
Joachim Andersen, September 2, 1903, September 20, 1903,
September 16, 1906, and at a Benefit concert, September 14, 1906.
See Biography, pp. 21 and 34.

W29

Op. 49 **PIRUN POLSKA** (POLKA DU DIABLE)
INTRODUCTION AND CAPRICE SUR DES AIRS FINNOIS
[d minor → D major]
(flute with piano or orchestral accompaniment)

First edition: Hamburg, Max Leichssenring, n.d. (Plate no. 782)
Andersen's copy is housed at the New York Public Library (vol. 2
of complete works); Danish Royal Library houses a second first-
edition copy.

Subsequent editions: Rühle & Wendling
(No longer in print)

Dedication: "A Madame Maria Landeker"

Selected performances: Joachim Andersen with the Berlin Philharmonic Orchestra, conducted by Gustav Kogel, September 1, 1890 (Première), September 19, 1890, October 8, 1890, January 25, 1891, and July 5, 1891.

Additional information: Danish Royal Library catalogue card provides date of 1892, and adds in parentheses that the work is for flute with piano or flute with an eighteen-member orchestra.

W30
Op. 50   **SCHWEDISCHE POLSKA-LIEDER** (by Isidore Dannström)
#1 D minor
(Plate no. 11568)
#2 G major
(Plate no. 11569)
#3 E minor
(Plate no. 11570)
#4 C major
(Plate no. 11571)
#5 D minor
(Plate no. 11572)
#6 F major
(Plate no. 11573)
(Transcriptions for flute with piano accompaniment)

First edition: Copenhagen, Wilhelm Hansen, n.d.
Andersen's copy is housed at the New York Public Library (vol. 3 of complete works); Danish Royal Library houses a second first-edition copy.

Publication contract: Signed with the Wilhelm Hansen Publishing Company, Copenhagen, December 18, 1894 (B14)
(150 crowns for this piece)

Subsequent editions: None
(Available in photocopy of the first edition)

Dedication: No. 1 & 2 Fräulein Fanny Christensen
(Fanny Christensen was a student of Joachim Andersen at the
Orchestra School.) See Biography, pp. 18 and 21.
        No. 3 & 4 Herrn Albert Zuge
        No. 5 & 6 Herrn Ernst Andersen
(Ernst Andersen was the son of Joachim Andersen and his first
wife, Emma Christina Jansson.) See Biography, p. 3.

Additional information: An announcement in the *Politiken* of July 22,
1895 (B20), stated that Andersen's works would be increased with
the addition of five new opus numbers during the year. The list
included six Swedish polskas. A second announcement in the
Dannebrog of August 8, 1896 (B19), stated that the pieces had just
been published by Wilhelm Hansen.

W31

Op. 51 **QUATRE MORCEAUX DE SALON**
#1 L'Attente (Die Erwartung) [A^b major]
#2 Intermezzo [b minor]
#3 Consolation (Tröstüng) [A major]
#4 Valse [F major]
(flute with piano accompaniment)

First edition: Hamburg, Max Leichssenring, n.d. (Plate no. 784)
Andersen's copy is housed at the New York Public Library (vol. 4
of complete works); Danish Royal Library houses a second first-
edition copy.

Subsequent editions: Rühle & Wendling, Southern in *Romantic Music
for Flute and Piano*, Book 1; "Intermezzo" published by Carl
Fischer, Cundy-Bettoney individually and in *Pleasures of Pan*, vol. 5

Dedication: "A Madame Adele Tieftrunk"

Selected performances: "Intermezzo" was performed by Ary van
Leeuwen (student of Joachim Andersen and principal flutist of the
Vienna Opera), June 28, 1905, in Tivoli Concert Hall with Holger
Dahl, pianist. See Biography, p. 9.

Additional information: Danish Royal Library catalogue card provides
date of 1892.

W32
Op. 52 **DREI SALONSTÜCKE**, I^{tes} Heft
#1 Melodie [B^b major]
(Plate no. 838)
#2 Wiegenlied [E^b major]
(Plate no. 839)
#3 Schmetterling, Intermezzo [G major]
(Plate no. 840)
(flute with piano accompaniment)

First edition: Hamburg, Max Leichssenring, n.d.
    Andersen's copy is housed at the New York Public Library (vol. 4
    of complete works); Danish Royal Library houses a second first-
    edition copy.

Subsequent editions: Rühle & Wendling; "Melodie" published by
    Oxford University Press in *Five Songs Without Words*
    (All pieces except the first are no longer in print.)

Dedication: "Meiner Schwägerin Mrs. Wm. C. Chapin verehrungsvoll
    zugeeignet"
    [Dedicated with respect to my sister-in-law, Mrs. William C. Chapin]

Additional information: Danish Royal Library catalogue card provides
    date of 1894.

VIER SALONSTÜCKE, II^{tes} Heft
#1 Pastorale [G major]
(Plate no. 851)
#2 Tanzlied [e minor]
(Plate no. 852)
#3 Idylle [E major]
(Plate no. 853)
#4 Jagdstück [D major]
(Plate no. 854)
(flute with piano accompaniment)

First edition: Hamburg, Max Leichssenring, n.d.
    Andersen's copy is housed at the New York Public Library (vol. 4
    of complete works); Danish Royal Library houses a second first-
    edition copy.

Subsequent editions: Rühle & Wendling
    (No longer in print)

Dedication: "Herrn William Maxwell zugeeignet"
[Dedicated to Mr. William Maxwell]

W33
Op. 53 **Canzone** [F major]
(Plate no. 836)
Erinnerung, Salonstück [B^b major]
(Plate no. 837)
(flute with piano accompaniment)

First edition: Hamburg, Max Leichssenring, n.d.
Andersen's copy is housed at the New York Public Library (vol. 4
of complete works); Danish Royal Library houses a second first-
edition copy.

Subsequent editions: Rühle & Wendling; "Canzone" published by Carl
Fischer, Cundy-Bettoney in *Pleasures of Pan*, vol. 6
(No longer in print)

Dedication: #1 "Miss Amy Whitman gewidmet"
[Dedicated to Miss Amy Whitman]
#2 "Miss May Bleecker gewidmet"
[Dedicated to Miss May Bleecker]

Additional information: Danish Royal Library catalogue card provides
date of 1894 for each piece.

W34
Op. 54 **DEUXIÈME IMPROMPTU** [A^b major]
(flute with piano accompaniment)

N. B. Andersen's first *Impromptu* is opus 7.

First edition: Hamburg, Max Leichssenring, n.d. (Plate no. 876)
Andersen's copy is housed at the New York Public Library (vol. 2
of complete works); Danish Royal Library houses a second first-
edition copy.

Subsequent editions: Rühle & Wendling, Southern in *Romantic Music
for Flute and Piano*, Book 2

Dedication: "Aux Frères Alfred et Philip Halstead"
[To brothers Alfred and Philip Halstead]

Selected performances: Jay Plowe in Tivoli Concert Hall, September 6, 1899. This was the first performance of the piece in Tivoli. See Biography, p. 9.

W35

Op. 55   **ACHT VORTRAGSSTÜCKE**
#1 Elegie [d minor]
(Plate no. 2069)
#2 Walzer [G major]
(Plate no. 2070)
#3 Notturno [B^b major]
(Plate no. 2071)
#4 Die Mühle [D major]
(Plate no. 2072)
#5 Legende [c minor]
(Plate no. 2073)
#6 Scherzino [D major]
(Plate no. 2074)
#7 Albumblatt [A major]
(Plate no. 2075)
#8 Tarantella [e minor]
(Plate no. 2076)
(flute with piano accompaniment)

First edition: Leipzig, Jules Heinrich Zimmermann, #1 & 8 1893, #2-7 1894
Andersen's copy is housed at the New York Public Library (vol. 4 of complete works); Danish Royal Library houses a second first-edition copy.

Subsequent editions: "Elegie" published by Rubank, European American Music Corp. in *The Andersen Collection*; "Die Mühle" published by Southern in *24 Short Concert Pieces*; "Legende" published by Southern; "Scherzino" published by Belwin, Billaudot, Consolidated Music Publishing, Cundy-Bettoney, Rubank, Southern in *24 Short Concert Pieces*; "Scherzino" arranged for flute quartet with the title *Valsette*, published by Belwin; All movements arranged for flute and guitar, published by Jim Roberts.

Dedication: None

Selected performances: "Legende" was performed by Johannes Ahlquist (student of Joachim Andersen) on an Orchestra School program at the Odd-Fellow Palace, May 8, 1904. See Biography, p. 21. (This piece was paired with the "Babillard" of op. 24.) "Scherzino" and "Albumblatt" were performed by Fanny Christensen (student of Joachim Andersen) with the Tivoli Orchestra, conducted by Joachim Andersen, September 14, 1898. See Biography, pp. 18 and 21. "Scherzino" was performed by Ary van Leeuwen (student of Joachim Andersen and principal flutist of the Vienna Opera) with Holger Dahl, pianist, in Tivoli Concert Hall, July 1, 1905, and again later in 1905, but with no date provided on the program. (On these occasions, van Leeuwen performed the work between his own "Danksagung," op. 19, no. 4, and "Vals" af *Suiten*, op. 116, by Benjamin Godard.) See Biography, p. 9.

Additional information: The Danish Royal Library's first-edition copy lists the date of publication as 1894 for all eight pieces.

W36

Op. 56 **FÜNF LEICHTERE STÜCKE**
   #1 Im Herbst [C major]
   (Plate no. 2117)
   #2 Die Blumen [G major]
   (Plate no. 2118)
   #3 Unterm Balkon [b minor]
   (Plate no. 2119)
   #4 Abendlied [F major]
   (Plate no. 2120)
   #5 Aus vergangenen Zeiten, Intermezzo [d minor]
   (Plate no. 2121)
   (flute with piano accompaniment)

First edition: Leipzig, Jules Heinrich Zimmermann, 1894
   Andersen's copy is housed at the New York Public Library (vol. 4 of complete works).

Subsequent editions: Rühle & Wendling; "Im Herbst" published by Southern; "Die Blumen" published by Southern, European American Music Corp. in *The Andersen Collection*; "Abendlied" published by Southern; "Aus vergangenen Zeiten" published by Cundy-Bettoney in *Pleasures of Pan*, vol. 6
   ("Unterm Balkon" and "Aus vergangenen Zeiten" are no longer in print)

Dedication: "Herrn E. C. Richardson gewidmet"
[Dedicated to Mr. E. C. Richardson]

W 37

Op. 57 **TROIS MORCEAUX**
#1 Le Calme, Romance [E^b major]
(Plate no. 11376)
#2 Sérénade Mélancolique [a minor]
(Plate no. 11377)
#3 Le Tourbillon [A major]
(Plate no. 11378)
(flute with piano accompaniment)

First edition: Copenhagen, Wilhelm Hansen, n.d.
Andersen's copy is housed at the New York Public Library (vol. 4
of complete works); Danish Royal Library houses a second first-
edition copy.

Publication contract: Signed with the Wilhelm Hansen Publishing
Company, July 28, 1893, titled "Stykker For Flute" (B14)
(125 crowns for this piece)

Subsequent editions: "Sérénade Mélancolique" published by Cundy-
Bettoney in *Pleasures of Pan*, vol. 6; "Le Tourbillon" published
by Southern
("Le Calme" and "Sérénade Mélancolique" are no longer in print.)

Dedication: "Dedié à ma belle soeur Mme. M. A. Stone"
[Dedicated to my sister-in-law, Mrs. M. A. Stone]

Selected performances: "Le Tourbillon" was performed by Robert
Enevoldsen in Tivoli Concert Hall, September 19, 1904
(Enevoldsen performed this work paired with the "Andante" from
Concerto in D Minor by Molique), and September 15, 1906.
See Biography, pp. 21 and 34.

Additional information: An announcement in the *Dannebrog* of April
24, 1894 (B19), stated that a new composition, op. 57, by Joachim
Andersen would be published by Wilhelm Hansen. Danish Royal
Library catalogue card provides date of 1894.

W 38

Op. 58 **INTRODUCTION ET CAPRICE SUR DES AIRS HONGROISES** [e minor → E major]
(flute with piano or orchestral accompaniment)

First edition: Copenhagen, Wilhelm Hansen, n.d. (Plate no. 11684)
Andersen's copy is housed at the New York Public Library (vol. 2 of complete works); Danish Royal Library houses a second first-edition copy.

Publication contract: Signed with the Wilhelm Hansen Publishing Company, Copenhagen, February 24, 1894 (B14)
(125 crowns for this piece)

Subsequent editions: None

Dedication: "A Monsieur Emil Prill"
(Emil Prill was a flute student of Joachim Andersen and, beginning in 1891, principal flutist of the Berlin Royal Opera.) See Biography, pp. 9 10.

Selected performances: There are two citations for performances of *Caprice*. One was a performance by Jay Plowe in Tivoli Concert Hall, September 6, 1899. This was the piece's first performance in Tivoli. See Biography, p. 9. *Kaprice* was performed by Robert Enevoldsen and the Tivoli Orchestra, September 15, 1906. See Biography, pp. 21 and 34.

Additional information: An announcement in the *Politiken* of July 22, 1895 (B20), stated that Joachim Andersen's works would be increased with the addition of five new opus numbers during the year. The list included op. 58, which would be published by Wilhelm Hansen.

W39

Op. 59 **FANTAISIES   NATIONALES**
#1 Danois [D major]
(Plate no. 11678)
#2 Ecossais [G major]
(Plate no. 11679)
#3 Russe [g minor → G major]
(Plate no. 11680)
#4 Suédois [d minor → D major]
(Plate no. 11681)
#5 Italien [A major]
(Plate no. 11682)
#6 Hongrois [a minor → A major]
(Plate no. 11683)
(flute with piano accompaniment)

First edition: Copenhagen, Wilhelm Hansen, n.d.
Andersen's copy is housed at the New York Public Library except
for the piano score of #5 (vol. 3 of complete works); Danish Royal
Library houses a second first-edition copy.

Publication contract: Signed with the Wilhelm Hansen Publishing
Company, Copenhagen, June 9, 1895 (B14)
(70 crowns for this piece; 570 crowns added for this work and opus
61)

Subsequent editions: None
(Available in photocopy of the first edition)

Dedication: None

Selected performances: "Ecossais" was performed by Christian Agerup
(student of Joachim Andersen) on an Orchestra School program,
March 10, 1901. See Biography, p. 21. "Italien" was performed
by Fanny Christensen (student of Joachim Andersen) at the German-
Nordic Exhibition of Trade and Industry in Lübeck, Germany,
August 4, 1895. See Biography, pp. 18 and 21.

Additional information: Publication contract lists the works differently: Dansk, Stokst, Italienne, Russisk, Svensk, and Hungarnsk. An announcement in the *Politiken* of July 22, 1895 (B20), stated that Andersen's works would be increased with the addition of five new opus numbers during the year. The list included six fantasies based on folk tunes. A second announcement in the *Dannebrog* of August 8, 1896 (B19), stated that the pieces had just been published by Wilhelm Hansen. The announcement stated that they are arrangements of folk tunes and are "tasteful and not very difficult."

W40

Op. 60 **SCHULE DER VIRTUOSITÄT**, 24 GROSSE STUDIEN
[All major and minor keys]
(flute alone)

First edition: Leipzig, Jules Heinrich Zimmermann, 1895
Andersen's copy is housed at the New York Public Library (vol. 1 of complete works); Danish Royal Library houses a second first-edition copy of vol. 1 of the etudes.

Subsequent editions: Belwin Mills, Billaudot, International, Kalmus, Presser, Southern; Three of the etudes published by Ricordi in *Tre Studi di Virtuosità*

Dedication: "Dem Andersen seines Bruders Vigo Andersen"
[To Andersen's brother Vigo Andersen] See Biography, pp. 18-19.

Additional information: Metronome markings are included in Joachim Andersen's copy.

W41

Op. 61 **DEUXIÈME MORCEAU DE CONCERT** [g minor → G major]
(flute with piano or orchestral accompaniment)

N. B. Andersen's first concert piece is *Concertstück*, op. 3.

First edition: Copenhagen, Wilhelm Hansen, n.d. (Plate no. 11763)
Andersen's copy is housed at the New York Public Library (vol. 2 of complete works); Danish Royal Library houses a second first-edition copy.

Publication contract: Signed with the Wilhelm Hansen Publishing
Company, Copenhagen, June 9, 1895 (B14)
(150 crowns for this piece; 570 crowns added for this piece and opus
59)

Subsequent editions: Wilhelmina (fl. & orch.)
(No longer in print)

Dedication: "A Monsieur Paul Taffanel"
(Paul Taffanel was Professor of Flute at the Paris Conservatory
between 1893 and 1908.) See Biography, pp. 11-12 and 14.

Selected performances: *Zweites Concertstück* was performed by Fanny
Christensen (student of Joachim Andersen) at the German-Nordic
Exhibition of Trade and Industry in Lübeck, Germany, August 4,
1895. See Biography, pp. 18 and 21. An announcement in the
Dannebrog of February 25, 1896 (B19), stated that the piece would be
performed by Peter Mollerup at the next Palace Concert. An announcement in the *Dannebrog* of August 19, 1896 (B19), stated that
the piece would be performed at the Crystal Palace by Albert Françella
and in Nuremberg by Wilhelm Tieftrunk. See Biography, pp. 7-8.

Additional information: An announcement in the *Dannebrog* of May 9,
1895 (B19), stated that Andersen had received a request from Mr.
Taffanel to compose a piece. This composition was selected as the
examination piece for the Paris Conservatory's *concours* in 1897.

W42
Op. 62 **QUATRE MORCEAUX**
#1 Cavatine [G major]
(Plate no. 12043)
#2 Intermezzo [D major]
(Plate no. 12044)
#3 Dans la Gondole [A major]
(Plate no. 12045)
#4 Sérénade d'Amour [a minor]
(Plate no. 12046)
(flute with piano accompaniment)

First edition: Copenhagen, Wilhelm Hansen, n.d.
Andersen's copy (flute parts and incomplete piano parts—#2, 3, 4
only) are housed at the New York Public Library (vol. 4 of complete works); Danish Royal Library houses a second first-edition
copy of #1 - 4.

Publication contract: Signed with the Wilhelm Hansen Publishing Company, Copenhagen, May 16, 1907 with the title *Quatre Morceaux* (B14)
(1000 crowns for this piece and six others)

Subsequent editions: None
(No longer in print)

Dedication: None

Additional information: An announcement in the *Dannebrog* of May 16, 1896 (B19), stated that Andersen was working on ten character pieces for flute and piano to be published by Wilhelm Hansen. The six additional pieces (#5 Danse orientale, #6 Nocturne, #7 Caprice, #8 L'Abeille, #9 Rêverie, and #10 Danse Espagnole) were abandoned.

W43
Op. 63   **ETUDES TECHNIQUES**   [All major and minor keys]
(flute alone)

First edition: Copenhagen, Wilhelm Hansen, n.d.
Andersen's copy is housed at the New York Public Library (vol. 1 of complete works); Danish Royal Library houses a second first-edition copy.

Publication contract: Signed with the Wilhelm Hansen Publishing Company, Copenhagen, May 16, 1907 (B14)
(1000 crowns for this piece and six others)

Subsequent editions: Bèrben, Billaudot, Edu-tainment, International, Kalmus, Salabert, Schirmer, Southern; Three of the etudes published by Ricordi in *Tre studi tecnini*

Dedication: Albert Françella

Additional information: Metronome markings are included in Joachim Andersen's copy.

Compositions without Opus Numbers

Cadenzas

W44
THREE CADENZAS
For the Flute Concerto in D Major, K. 314 (Mozart)

First edition: Breitkopf & Härtel
A first-edition copy is housed at the New York Public Library;
Danish Royal Library houses a second first-edition copy.

Subsequent editions: Ashley Publications, Cundy-Bettoney, Southern,
Amsco in *Selected Flute Solos*

Additional information: New York Public Library catalogue card
indicates that the Breitkopf & Härtel edition was "reprinted from
plates of 1886."

W45
CADENZAS for **LE CARNAVAL RUSSE** (by César Ciardi)

First edition: Unknown

Subsequent editions: Simrock

Performances: Joachim Andersen performed this piece at the inaugural
concert of the Berlin Philharmonic Orchestra, October 17, 1882.
See Biography, p. 5. He also performed the work with the Berlin
Philharmonic Orchestra, conducted by Gustav Kogel, November 6,
1887, April 2, 1888, April 22, 1888, June 28, 1888, November 4,
1888, January 20, 1889, September 15, 1890, November 16, 1890,
February 15, 1891, June 16, 1891, and September 29, 1891, and
with the Berlin Philharmonic Orchestra, conducted by Franz
Mannstädt, April 28, 1886, December 26, 1886, May 19, 1887,
June 1, 1887, June 3, 1887, and June 5, 1887. Franz Schmeling
performed this piece with the Berlin Philharmonic Orchestra, conducted by Rudolph Herfurth, April 10, 1892.

Piano Compositions

W46
KONG CHRISTIAN X. HONNØR-MARSCH [F major]
(piano solo)

First edition: Copenhagen, Wilhelm Hansen, n.d. (Plate no. 13853)
Andersen's copy is housed at the New York Public Library; Danish
Royal Library houses a second first-edition copy.

Publication contract: Signed with the Wilhelm Hansen Publishing
Company, Copenhagen, May 16, 1907 (B14)
(1000 crowns for this piece and six others)

Arrangements: Violin solo, violin and piano, chamber orchestra, and
full orchestra

Subsequent editions: None

Dedication: "Hans Majestaet Kongen tilegnet som Kronprins"
[Dedicated to his Majesty the Crown Prince]

Performances: Orchestral transcription performed by the Tivoli Orchestra,
conducted by Joachim Andersen, May 11, 1906, May 17, 1906,
May 20, 1906, May 24, 1906, May 31, 1906, June 4, 1906, July 6,
1906, July 13, 1906, August 12, 1906, June 2, 1907, July 9, 1907,
August 4, 1907, and September 8, 1907; Performed at Rosenborg
Gardens, conducted by Joachim Andersen, June 4, 1906, June 23,
1907, June 14, 1908, July 26, 1908, and July 27, 1908; Performed
at a Folk Concert, conducted by Joachim Andersen, June 24, 1906.

Additional information: The Danish Royal Library houses parts for the
orchestral arrangement [Wilhelm Hansen, Plate no. 15180]

W47
PAA HURTIGPRESSE.   MARSCH-POLKA [D major]
(piano solo)

First edition: Copenhagen, Wilhelm Hansen, n.d. (Plate no. 12060)
Andersen's copy is housed at the New York Public Library; Danish
Royal Library houses a second first-edition copy.

Subsequent editions: None
(No longer in print)

Dedication: "Journalistforeningen tilegnet"
[Dedicated to the Journalism Society]

Additional information: [1899?] is handwritten on the cover page of
Andersen's copy.

W48
POLONAISE [D major]
(piano solo)

First edition: Copenhagen, Wilhelm Hansen, n.d. or plate no.
Andersen's copy is housed at the New York Public Library.

Subsequent editions: None
(No longer in print)

Dedication: "komponeret i Anledning af Peter de Nully Brown's
Fodselsdag 2 April 1899"
[Composed for the occasion of Peter de Nully Brown's birthday,
April 2, 1899]

W49
SØLVMYRTER. VALS FOR PIANO [C major]
(piano solo)

First edition: Copenhagen, Wilhelm Hansen, n.d. (Plate no. 12001)
Andersen's copy is housed at the New York Public Library.

Subsequent editions: None
(No longer in print)

Dedication: "Hr. Bankier N. Thomsen og Hustru tilegnet"
[Dedicated to Banker N. Thomson and his wife]

Additional information: [ca. 1898] is handwritten on the cover page of
Andersen's copy. A cover page housed at the Music History
Museum in Copenhagen (B7) includes a handwritten dedication
from Andersen to Sophie Claudius, dated Copenhagen, June 10,
1897.

W50
SLARAFFIA-MAZURKA [d minor]
(piano solo)

First edition: Copenhagen, Wilhelm Hansen, n.d. (Plate no. 12061)
    A first-edition copy is housed at the New York Public Library;
    Danish Royal Library houses a second first-edition copy.

Subsequent editions: None
    (No longer in print)

Dedication: "Kunstnerforeningen af 18 Novbr. tilegnet"
    [Dedicated to the Artist Union on November 18th]

Additional information: [1899?] is handwritten on the cover page of
    Andersen's copy.

Cornet and Piano

W51
ALBUMBLATT
(cornet with piano accompaniment)

First edition: Hamburg, Max Leichssenring, n.d. (Plate no. 801)
    A first-edition copy is housed at the New York Public Library.

Subsequent editions: None
    (No longer in print)

Dedication: None

Additional information: New York Public Library catalogue card
    provides date of "ca. 1888."

Transcriptions

W52

ANDANTE FUNEBRE (for orchestra) by Johan S. Svendsen
Arranged for flute with piano accompaniment by Joachim Andersen

First edition: Copenhagen, Wilhelm Hansen, n.d.
    Andersen's copy is housed at the New York Public Library (vol. 4
    of complete works).

Publication contract: Signed with the Wilhelm Hansen Publishing
    Company, Copenhagen, May 16, 1907 (B14)
    (1000 crowns for this piece and six others)

Subsequent editions: None
    (No longer in print)

Dedication: None

W53

EINZUGSMARSCH DER BOJAREN (for orchestra) by Johan
Halvorsen
Arranged for flute with piano accompaniment by Joachim Andersen

First edition: Copenhagen, Wilhelm Hansen, n.d.
    Andersen's copy is housed at the New York Public Library (vol. 4
    of complete works).

Publication contract: Signed with the Wilhelm Hansen Publishing
    Company, Copenhagen, May 16, 1907 (B14)
    (1000 crowns for this piece and six others)

Subsequent editions: None
    (No longer in print)

Dedication: None

W54

RESIGNATION by V. Neupert, op. 26, no. 1

First edition: Copenhagen, Wilhelm Hansen, n.d.

Publication contract: Signed with the Wilhelm Hansen Publishing
    Company, Copenhagen, May 16, 1907 (B14)
    (1000 crowns for this piece and six others)

Subsequent editions: None
    (No longer in print)

Dedication: None

Unpublished Manuscripts

W55
98 POSTHUMOUS EXERCISES AND PRELUDES

Manuscript: Housed at the Music History Museum in Copenhagen
    (B7)

Facsimile edition: Autographus Musicus, Stockholm, 1989. (B34)

Subsequent editions: Wilhelm Hansen as *100 Posthumous Studies &
    Preludes*

Dedication: None

THEORI Manuscript

Manuscript date: February 5, 1901
Housed at the Danish Royal Library. See Biography, p. 32. (B6)

Discography

Flute Compositions

D 1

Adorján, András, flutist, and Christian Ivaldi, pianist. *Fantaisie Hongroise.*
Tudor 756, 1992.
> Op. 59, no. 6 "Hongrois" (7 minutes, 50 seconds)

D 2

Bennett, William, Toke Lund Christiansen, Jens Bøje Hansen, Michie Bennett,
flutists. *Syrinx: Music for 1.2.3.4 Flutes.* EMI 27 0486 1, 1986.
> Op. 30, no. 23 (3 minutes, 23 seconds)

D 3

Christiansen, Toke Lund, flutist, and Per Salo, pianist. *Morceaux pour la Flûte
avec accompagnement de Piano par Joachim Andersen.* Kontrapunkt 32079,
1991.
> Op. 7   (6 minutes, 11 seconds)
> Op. 44 (4 minutes, 53 seconds)
> Op. 45, no. 2 "Norma" (10 minutes, 52 seconds)
> Op. 55
>> No. 1 "Elegie" (4 minutes, 58 seconds)
>> No. 2 "Walzer" (3 minutes, 36 seconds)
>> No. 3 "Notturno" (3 minutes, 59 seconds)
>> No. 4 "Die Mühle" (3 minutes, 12 seconds)
>> No. 5 "Legende" (6 minutes, 46 seconds)
>> No. 6 "Scherzino" (1 minute, 45 seconds)
>> No. 7 "Albumblatt" (4 minutes, 24 seconds)
>> No. 8 "Tarantella" (1 minute, 47 seconds)
> Op. 56
>> No. 3 "Unterm Balkon" (1 minute, 52 seconds)
>> No. 4 "Abendlied" (3 minutes, 34 seconds)

Op. 57
No. 1 "Le Calme" (5 minutes, 39 seconds)
No. 3 "Le Tourbillon" (3 minutes, 39 seconds)

D 4

Fromanger, Benoit, flutist, and Jean-Yves Sebillotte, pianist. *Musica Fantasca XIXe*. Forlane UCD 16574, 1988.
Op. 50
No. 2 (2 minutes, 40 seconds)
No. 3 (4 minutes, 56 seconds)
No. 5 (3 minutes, 19 seconds)
No. 6 (3 minutes, 13 seconds)

D 5

Peck, Donald, flutist, and Melody Lord, pianist. Boston Records BR1010CD, 1994.
Op. 55, no. 6 "Scherzino"

D 6

Robison, Paula, flutist, and Samuel Sanders, pianist. *Grieg & Andersen: Music for Flute and Piano*. Arabesque Recordings Z6668, 1995.
Op. 7 (5 minutes, 22 seconds)
Op. 9 (4 minutes, 38 seconds)
Op. 24
No. 1 "Chant Pastorale" (2 minutes, 24 seconds)
No. 2 "Rêverie" (3 minutes, 5 seconds)
No. 3 "Alla Mazurka" (3 minutes, 17 seconds)
No. 6 "Babillard" (2 minutes, 35 seconds)
Op. 28, no. 1 "Berceuse" (3 minutes, 34 seconds)
Op. 52, no. 1 "Melodie" (1 minute, 58 seconds)
Op. 55
No. 4 "Die Mühle" (2 minutes, 52 seconds)
No. 8 "Tarantella" (1 minute, 30 seconds)
Op. 56, no. 2 "Die Blumen" (2 minutes, 19 seconds)

D 7

Sebon, Karl-Bernard, flutist, Radio-Symphonie-Orchester Berlin, Uros Lajovic. Koch 3-1313-2, 1982.
Cadenzas for César Ciardi's *Le Carnaval Russe* (7 minutes, 15 seconds)

D 8

Wegner, Hans-Jörg, flutist, and Christiane Kroeker, pianist. *Flöten-Fantasien.* Thorofon CTH 2187, 1993.

> Op. 55, no. 1 "Elegie" (3 minutes, 9 seconds)
> Cadenzas for César Ciardi's *Le Carnaval Russe* (6 minutes, 53 seconds)

Flute Recordings No Longer in Print

D 9

Bennett, Harold, flutist. *Harold Bennett Demonstrates and Discusses Andersen, op. 33, Debussy, Syrinx.* Winds of the World Records JFEC 22586, 1986.

> Op. 33

D 10

Blaisdell, Frances, Harry Moskovitz, Murray Panitz, James Pellerite, Frederick Wilkins, flutists, and Moreland Kortkamp, pianist. *Flutists' Showcase.* Golden Crest Records CR 4020.

> Op. 55, no. 6 "Scherzino" (arranged for three flutes in C and piano)

D 11

Kincaid, William, flutist, and Vladimir Sokoloff, pianist. *William Kincaid Plays the Flute.* Award Artists Series, Grand Award Records AAS-705.

> Op. 55, no. 6 "Scherzino"

D 12

Moskovitz, Harry, flutist. *The Flute Family.* Mark Records 23396.

> Op. 33, no. 6 (alto flute)

D 13

Moyse, Marcel, flutist. *Flute Playing by the Great Flutist 1,* "The French Flute School at Home." Marcel Moyse Records M99, 195? and Maramatsu Records MGF 1001.

> Op. 15, no. 3, 4, 8, 15, 16, and 18.

D 14

Peck, Donald, flutist. *24 Exercises for the Flute, op. 33.* Armstrong/Edutainment, 1976.

> Op. 33

D15

Pellerite, James J., flutist, and Dr. Charles Webb, Jr., pianist. *The Flute in its Showcase of Styles*. Golden Crest Records in cooperation with Southern Music RE 7023.
>   Op. 56, no. 4 "Abendlied"

D16

Penville, Edith, flutist, and Roland Renvell, pianist. Columbia 2684-D.
>   Op. 16 -- This recording is an abridged version of the first-edition score.

D17

Thomas, Mark, flutist, and Russell Woollen, pianist/harpsichordist. *Flute Recital*, Vol. II. Armstrong/Edu-tainment F500-4.
>   Op. 55, no. 6 "Scherzino"

Other Compositions

D18

Musik for konge og folk. Historical recordings by the Band of Music of The Royal Danish Life Guards. EMI Classics 5552482, 1994.
>   Kong Christian X. Honnør-Marsch (2 minutes, 30 seconds)

Annotated Bibliography

Primary Sources

Documents and Collections

B1

Andersen, Joachim. Compositions. Catalogued separately by individual titles. Music Division, The Royal Library, Copenhagen, Denmark.

Extensive collection of Joachim Andersen's music. While a number of compositions are missing (op. 16; op. 23; op. 24; op. 33; op. 45, no. 2, 6, and 8; op. 56; op. 60, vol. 2; *Le Carnaval Russe* cadenza; *Polonaise* [piano solo]; *Sølvmyrter* [piano solo]; *Albumblatt* [cornet with piano accompaniment]; and Andersen's three transcriptions), it is the second largest public collection of first-edition copies of Andersen scores in the world. As noted in the Catalogue of Compositions, handwritten markings by Andersen have been added to two of the pieces, *Moto Perpetuo*, op. 8, and *La Résignation et Polonaise*, op. 22.

B2

Andersen, Joachim. *Compositions for Flute and Piano*. Music Division, New York Public Library for the Performing Arts.

Largest public collection of first-edition copies of Joachim Andersen's music. Donated by Andersen's widow, Sarah Dana Watson Andersen, the collection contains Andersen's personal scores of all of his flute and piano compositions except the piano score for "Russe," op. 59, no. 3, the piano score for "Cavatine," op. 62, no. 1, and the cadenza for Ciardi's *Le Carnaval Russe*. The Music Division of the New York Public Library for the Performing Arts also owns Andersen's five compositions for solo piano and the *Albumblatt* for cornet and piano, which are catalogued separately by composer and title.

B3

Andersen, Joachim. "Curriculum Vitae," November 16, 1905, Royal Palace,
    Copenhagen, Denmark.

Two-and-a-half-page chronological narrative handwritten (in Danish) by Andersen
just after he was knighted by the Danish royalty. Most notably, he writes of a
"vicious tongue disease caused by exhaustion in 1892," then notes, "I returned to
Copenhagen in the fall of 1895, the same year as my first Palace Concerts took
place." (He does not mention anything about the years 1892 to 1895.) Andersen
states that he is the composer of sixty-three works (exercises and concert pieces)
for flute and piano or orchestral accompaniment and that he has had "the
satisfaction of knowing that my music has not only found its way into the
concert hall, but is also being used for educational purposes in music
conservatories in Copenhagen and abroad." Andersen cites 1897 as the year he
founded the Orchestra School. While this was the year of the school's first
concert, articles in the *Dannebrog* newspaper (B19) announced the opening the
previous year.

B4

Andersen, (Karl) Joachim. "Letters." The Royal Library, Copenhagen, Denmark.

Collection of twenty-five handwritten letters by Andersen to various associates
including Carl Skjerne (principal clarinetist of the Palace and Tivoli orchestras),
Gustav Hetsch (music critic), Anton Svendsen (composer and conductor), Fritz
Bendix (pianist and conductor), Hakon Børresen (composer and student of Anton
Svendsen), Sextus Miskow (opera singer and teacher), Peter Nansen (author and
publisher), J. Moldenhauer (Chairman of the Institute for the Blind), Johann
Jacobsen and his wife, Mühlfeldt, and Jensen. The letters include invitations to
upcoming concerts, responses to correspondence, and directives regarding his
orchestras. Next to his signature on four of the letters, Andersen added clever
caricatures of himself. In each drawing, he is conducting in tails with his back
to the viewer, thereby showing the part in his hair which stretched down the
back of his head. The part was a favorite subject of cartoonists in Andersen's
day. (See Biography, pp. 23-24.) In addition to one of the drawings, on a letter
to Johann Jacobsen, dated May 27, 1897, Andersen included an autograph of the
first seven measures of his "Legende," op. 55, no. 5.

B5

Andersen, (Karl) Joachim. "Oversigt over Palæ-Koncerternes Repertoire ved de
    300 Koncerter (30 October 1895-28 February 1909)." Copenhagen, 1908-09.
    Pasted in vol. 6 of "Andersen, Joachim. Programs of circa 2400 orchestral

concerts conducted by Joachim Andersen in Scheveningen, 1890-92, Lübeck, 1895, and Copenhagen, 1894-1909." Compiled by Mrs. Joachim Andersen. Music Division, New York Public Library for the Performing Arts.

Thirty-one-page unpublished index of compositions performed at the Palace Concerts in Copenhagen, conducted by Joachim Andersen, between October 30, 1895, and February 28, 1909. The document provides an alphabetical list of pieces arranged by genre and an alphabetical list of soloists. Because one of the goals of the concert series was to provide an opportunity for the performance of Danish works, Danish composers and soloists are typed in bold print. This index can also be found in the first volume of "Franz Schnedler-Petersen's Scrapbooks," a collection of newspaper articles and related materials donated to the Music History Museum and Carl Claudius Collection in Copenhagen, Denmark. (B7) Franz Schnedler-Petersen was Andersen's successor as conductor of the Palace Concerts.

B 6

Andersen, Joachim. "Theori." Music Division, The Royal Library, Copenhagen, Denmark.

Unpublished theoretical treatise completed by Andersen in 1901. Each of the approximately one hundred pages contains handwritten musical examples, primarily counterpoint exercises, sometimes with narrative notes by Andersen. Most of the exercises are written in two or three voices.

B 7

"Andersen, Joachim. Collections." Music History Museum and Carl Claudius Collection, Copenhagen, Denmark.

One of the world's largest collections of Andersen materials, containing "Victor Gandrup's Collection about Joachim Andersen," "The Carl Claudius Collection of Musical Instruments," a file of Andersen photographs, and books and other items related to Andersen and Danish musical life at the turn of the century. Among the more recent acquisitions is "Joachim Andersen (1847-1909): Berliner Filharmoniens stifter, Fløjtens Chopin" (Joachim Andersen [1847-1909]: Berlin Philharmonic Founder, Chopin of the Flute), an unpublished article by Toke Lund Christiansen (currently Denmark's leading flutist), written for a 1997 exhibition honoring the 150th anniversary of Andersen's birth.

"Victor Gandrup's Collection about Joachim Andersen."

Handwritten notes collected and donated by Victor Gandrup (1891-1966), who was apparently preparing to write a biography of Andersen. Gandrup, an active collector of material concerning Danish music history, was a Conservatory student at the end of Andersen's life and later a violist, then concertmaster of the Royal Orchestra. The collection includes a copy of the contract Andersen used when employing musicians for his Palace Concerts and an autograph of a still largely unknown book of etudes. The etude collection has been published by Wilhelm Hansen (with alterations) as *100 Posthumous Studies & Preludes*, edited by Toke Lund Christiansen, and in a facsimile edition by Autographus Musicus, titled *98 Posthumous Exercises and Preludes*.

"Carl Claudius Collection of Musical Instruments."

Collection which contains the ivory baton Andersen received from the Board of Directors at the spa in Scheveningen, Holland, in 1892. After Andersen's death in 1909, his widow, Sarah Dana Watson Andersen, donated the baton to the Music History Museum and Carl Claudius Collection. The Holtzapfel one-keyed flute that Andersen played on a concert celebrating the opening of the Museum, February 6, 1898, is also part of the collection.

B8
"Andersen, (Karl) Joachim. Papers, 1882-1899." Special Collections Library, Duke University, Durham, North Carolina.

Forty-six letters, in French and German, written to Andersen between 1882 and 1899.
> Eleven letters (1883-1895) written by Paul Taffanel, flute professor at the Paris Conservatory. They include information about Andersen's *Concertstück*, op. 3, and *Ballade et Danse des Sylphes*, op. 5, tongue problems experienced by both Andersen and Taffanel, and meetings in Berlin. Andersen dedicated his *Impromptu*, op. 7, *Moto Perpetuo*, op. 8, and *Deuxième Morceau de Concert*, op. 61, to Taffanel.
> Two letters (1888) written by Jean Dumon, flute professor at the Brussels Conservatory, to whom Andersen dedicated his op. 37 collection of etudes.
> Eight letters (1882-1888) written by Wilhelm Barge, principal flutist of the Leipzig Gewandhaus Orchestra and flute professor at the music conservatory in Leipzig, to whom Andersen dedicated his *Tarantella*, op. 10.

One letter (1894) written by Wenzel Bukovsky, flute professor at the Royal
Music School in Würzburg.

Three letters (1890-1896) written by Albert Françella, flute professor at the
Guildhall School of Music, to whom Andersen dedicated his op. 63
collection of etudes.

Four letters (1883-1888) written by Moritz Fürstenau, flute professor at the
Dresden Conservatory, to whom Andersen dedicated his *Au Bord de
la Mer*, op. 9.

Six letters (1887-1890) written by Roman Kukula, flute professor at the
conservatory in Vienna, to whom Andersen dedicated his op. 30
collection of etudes.

Two letters (1889 and undated) from Oskar Kohler, conductor and teacher at
the Stern Conservatory in Berlin.

One letter (1887) written by Wilhelm Popp, principal flutist of the
Hamburg Philharmonic, to whom Andersen dedicated his *Variations
Drolatiques sur un air Suédois*, op. 26.

One letter (1899) written by Robert Seel, flutist of the U. S. Marine Band.

One letter (1891) written by Richard Unger, principal flutist of the resort
orchestra at Homburg-vor-der-Höhe.

Three letters (1883-1896) written by Theodor Winkler, Grand Ducal flute
chamber virtuoso and member of the Royal Chamber in Weimar.

Three letters (1882-1888) written by F. Waterstraat, flute professor at the
Imperial Russian Conservatory in St. Petersburg, to whom Andersen
dedicated his op. 21 collection of etudes.

B9

"Andersen, Joachim. Programs of circa 2400 orchestral concerts conducted by
Joachim Andersen in Scheveningen, 1890-92, Lübeck, 1895, and
Copenhagen, 1894-1909." Compiled by Mrs. Joachim Andersen. New
York, 1913. 6 vol. and 8 vol. of index. Music Division, New York Public
Library for the Performing Arts.

Collection of now-brittle scrapbooks compiled by Mrs. Joachim Andersen (Sarah
Dana Watson Andersen) between 1890 and 1909. Included in the collection are
concert programs, rosters of orchestral membership handwritten by Andersen,
newspaper articles, invitations to special events, and the "Oversigt over Palae-
Koncerternes Repertoire ved de 300 Koncerter (30 October-28 February 1909),"
which is pasted in volume six. (B5) Mrs. Andersen proudly collected all of the
items in this extensive compilation during her courtship and marriage, pasted
them carefully into scrapbooks, often adding personal handwritten comments,
and donated them to the New York Public Library, where she was an employee
after her husband's death.

B10

Berlin Philharmonic Orchestra Archive, National Institute for Music Research, Berlin, Germany.

Extensive collection of original programs of Berlin Philharmonic Orchestra concerts. Although many documents were destroyed during World War II, subsequent donations to the Archive have restored much of the collection. The archive also owns a large collection of books about the history of the orchestra.

B11

Chace, Laura. Letter to author, 27 July 1998. Author's collection.

Letter written by the Director of the Cincinnati Historical Society Library to report the results of research concerning the *Dannebrog* newspaper's (B19) account, dated May 9, 1895, that Andersen had been offered the position of conductor of the Cincinnati Symphony Orchestra. Chace did not find any mention of Andersen in connection with the Cincinnati Symphony. And, she reported that Frank Van der Stucken, the first conductor of the orchestra, had already received a contract from the Cincinnati Orchestra Association by April 12, 1895.

B12

"Clipping File, Joachim Andersen." Music Division, New York Public Library for the Performing Arts.

Letters of recommendation for Andersen and music reviews of performances in Copenhagen during the 1894-95 Palace Concert season. The recommendations were written by Hans von Bülow (eminent conductor under whom Andersen worked for five years), Joseph Joachim (virtuoso violinist and music director of the Berlin Hochschule), Edvard Grieg (renowned Norwegian composer), Johan Svendsen (composer and conductor), Martin Blumner (conductor of the Berlin Singacademie), Karl Klindworth (one of the Berlin Philharmonic's conductors), Moritz Moszkowski (pianist, composer, and teacher at the Kullak Academy in Berlin), Carl Mahns, M. A. Reiss (Executive Director of the spa in Scheveningen), and one letter jointly by L. Sacerdoti and P. Landeker (Berlin businessmen and Philharmonic supporters), during the period 1892 to 1895 when Andersen stopped performing and sought a full-time conducting position. According to Andersen's *curriculum vitae* (B3), these letters helped him secure the position of conductor of the German-Nordic Exhibition of Trade and Industry Orchestra (Lübeck) in 1895. Edvard Grieg wrote, "....I've known for some time that you were a flutist of first rank, but now, to my surprise, I realize that you are an excellent conductor who, in regular collaboration with an excellent orchestra, will contribute substantially to increasing the popularity of fine orchestral music...." And, Moritz Moszkowski stated, "It is certainly most regrettable that Joachim Andersen, whom Berlin musicians have always respected as the greatest living flute virtuoso, will no longer belong to the public in this role." The only other item in this file is a brief article about Andersen's "Scherzino," op. 55, no. 6, a program note which accompanied a performance by John Wummer (principal flutist of the New York Philharmonic).

B13

"Collection of Danish telegrams sent to Joachim Andersen, musical director at Copenhagen. Dated 1905-09." Art and Architecture Collection, New York Public Library.

Twenty-four telegrams, some with handpainted decorative designs, sent to Andersen during the years 1901, 1904, 1905, 1907, 1908, and 1909. Donated to the New York Public Library by Mrs. Joachim Andersen (Sarah Dana Watson Andersen) on March 12, 1913, the collection contains short congratulatory messages, including birthday greetings. Senders include Johannes Ahlquist (a flute student at the Orchestra School), Robert Enevoldsen (a flutist in Andersen's Palace and Tivoli orchestras), Georg K. Hansen, Thorvald and Anna Thrane, Yelva Wolf, Anton Bloch, Johan Svendsen (composer and conductor), Ella Carlsen, Axel Guldbrandsen, and Leocadie Gerlach.

B14

Publication contracts, Wilhelm Hansen Publishing Company, Copenhagen, Denmark.

Publication contracts Andersen signed with Copenhagen's leading music publisher between 1889 and 1907. These contracts are for the following compositions:
Op. 37 — Signed in Berlin, May 24, 1889
Op. 57 — Signed in Copenhagen, July 28, 1893
Op. 58 — Signed in Copenhagen, February 24, 1894
Op. 45 — Signed in Berlin, June 12, 1894
Op. 50 — Signed in Copenhagen, December 18, 1894
Op. 59 and op. 61 — Signed in Copenhagen, June 9, 1895
Op. 44, 62, 63, *Kong Christian X. Honnør-Marsch*, *Andante Funebre* (transcription), *Einzugsmarsch der Bojaren* (transcription), and *Resignation* (transcription) — Signed in Copenhagen, May 16, 1907

The publisher also has a postcard, mailed to the company from Staten Island, New York, June 13, 1928, which reads "Fru Joachim Andersen acknowledges with thanks receipt of Radio-Royalty checks for '27/'28 deposited in her account in Private Banken May 30th, 1928."

B15
Sink, Robert. Letter to author, 6 September 1996. Author's collection.

Brief letter written to the author by New York Public Library Archivist-Records Manager Robert Sink, describing Sarah Dana Watson Andersen's employment at the New York Public Library between 1910 and 1915. See Biography, p. 10.

Newspapers

B16
Berliner Tageblatt

Daily newspaper which published reviews of Berlin Philharmonic Orchestra concerts during Andersen's tenure with the orchestra.

B17
Berlinske Tidende, Den (Copenhagen)

One of the major daily Copenhagen newspapers. Founded in 1749, the paper published many articles about Palace, Tivoli, and Orchestra School concerts during the years 1894 through 1909 when Andersen was active in the city.

B18
Chicago Daily Tribune

"Suicide at a Soiree," 30 January 1895.

Lengthy article published at the time of Vigo Andersen's shocking suicide in 1895. The newspaper account describes details of the musical soiree he hosted on the night of his death, events leading up to the suicide, possible causes, and biographical information about Vigo, noting his contributions to the Chicago Orchestra. The author relies on hearsay and provides minute details of the evening's events. A portion of this article is quoted on page 19 of the Biography.

"Vigo Andersen's Mind Deranged," 31 January 1895.

Follow-up article which appeared after an inquest into the cause of Vigo Andersen's death. According to this report, the coroner's jury "returned a verdict of suicide while temporarily insane," having heard testimony from one of Vigo's children that Vigo "had suffered from mental derangement while he lived in Copenhagen."

B19
Dannebrog (Copenhagen)

Daily morning Copenhagen newspaper published from September 1, 1892, to November 3, 1910. During this time it was a competitor of the *Politiken* (B20), which survives. The *Dannebrog* published many announcements, reviews, and articles about Andersen and always treated him favorably.

"Populære Symfonikoncerter," 12 February 1894 — Announcement of the first two Palace Concerts, including their programs.

"Hans von Bülow og Joachim Andersen," 22 February 1894 — Article about Hans von Bülow's support during the onset of Andersen's tongue affliction and von Bülow's letter of recommendation written for Andersen in 1893.

"Joachim Andersen i Lübeck," 10 August 1895 — Report of Andersen's success as orchestral conductor at the German-Nordic Exhibition of Trade and Industry in Lübeck, Germany.

9 May 1895 — Announcement that Andersen had been offered a position as conductor of the Cincinnati Symphony. Research conducted by Laura Chace, Director of the Cincinnati Historical Society Library, shows that this was an erroneous report. (See B11.)

26 August 1896 — Introduction of the Orchestra School with reasons for its founding.

28 January 1898 — Interview with Andersen regarding his goals for the Tivoli Orchestra.

9 August 1909 — Disclosure of information about Andersen's final illness and death as described by his doctor.

B20
Politiken (Copenhagen)

Founded in 1884 as a protest paper, today one of Copenhagen's two major daily newspapers, the *Berlinske Tidende* (B17) being the other. Articles in the

Politiken between 1894 and 1909 included many reviews and related announcements about Palace, Tivoli, and Orchestra School concerts.

> Plutus, "Hos Joachim Andersen," 20 February 1894 — Article published on the eve of the inaugural Palace Concert to reintroduce the Copenhagen public to Andersen. (Addendum added the following day)
>
> "Joachim Andersen 1. Symphoni-Koncerter," 23 February 1894 — Review of Andersen's first Palace Concert.
>
> "Tivolis ny Dirigent," 27 January 1898 — Biographical article written at the time of Andersen's appointment as Tivoli's conductor.
>
> "Vinter Concerts og Palæ Concerts," 9 December 1898 — Article by Franz Schnedler-Petersen announcing the suspension of his winter orchestra concerts because Andersen would not allow Palace Concert musicians to play in Schnedler-Petersen's ensemble.
>
> "Palæ Concerts og Vinter Concerts," 20 December 1898 — Explanation of the conflict between Andersen and Schnedler-Petersen and a request for Andersen to respond to the accusation that he would not allow Palace orchestra members to play for Schnedler-Petersen.
>
> "Mr. Joachim Andersen og Vinter Concerts," 22 December 1898 — Response from Andersen and commentary by the *Politiken.*
>
> "Vinter Concerts og Palæ Concerts," 28 December 1898 — Letter from Schnedler-Petersen demanding that Andersen be direct in stating that he would allow his musicians to perform in Schnedler-Petersen's orchestra.
>
> "Orkester-Konflikten," 27 October 1904 — Formation of a Violinists' Union and demands by the Palace Concert musicians for increased salaries.
>
> "Orkesterkonflikten," 4 November 1904 — Interview with Andersen regarding the conflict with the musicians and a report that the Violinists' Union had agreed to give up their demands.
>
> "Orkesterkonflikten," 20 November 1904 — Dismissal of Concertmaster Hemme and the end of the orchestra conflict.
>
> "Joachim Andersen død," 8 May 1909 — Obituary.

B21
Vössische Zeitung (Berlin)

Daily Berlin newspaper which reviewed Berlin Philharmonic Orchestra concerts during Andersen's tenure with the orchestra.

Dissertations

B22

Dzapo, Kyle Jean. "Carl Joachim Andersen: A Biography and Study of His Compositions for Flute and Piano." D. M. thesis, Northwestern University, 1996.

Three-part document containing a biography, analysis of compositions for flute and piano, and catalogue of compositions. The biography is substantial, but has been augmented for the present volume. The analysis outlines general style characteristics of Andersen's music (Form, Melody, Harmony, and Rhythm and Meter) and includes many musical examples from his flute and piano works. The catalogue forms the basis for the one contained in this volume. Appendices provide representative concert programs in which Andersen participated as either flutist or conductor and little-known portraits, related photographs, and drawings.

B23

Fonville, John Winston. "A Pedagogical Approach to the Flute Etudes of Joachim Andersen." D. M. thesis, University of Illinois, 1981.

Large-scale study of Joachim Andersen's etudes. In his thesis, John Fonville argues that, while flutists generally study etudes in a sequential order, a more effective pedagogical method is to arrange etudes in progressive order with regard to specific, individual technical difficulties (for example, slurred scale patterns, slurred scale and interval patterns, slurred interval patterns, tongued duple rhythms, tongued triple rhythms, etc.) and study each technical problem using progressively more difficult etudes to reinforce "the essental phenomena of repetition and redundancy" before proceeding to the next. For each etude in the eight standard volumes of Andersen etudes, Fonville determines its primary technical challenge, groups it with others having the same challenge, then arranges it within the group according to level of difficulty.

B24

Jacobus, Rhea Beth. "The Literature of the French Flute School 1800-1880: Style Characteristics, Sociological Influences, and Pedagogical Applications." D. A. diss., Ball State University, 1990.

Study of six composers, Tulou, Boehm, Altes, Genin, Demersseman, and Andersen, who were also flute virtuosi during the nineteenth century. According to the author's abstract:

The years from 1800 to 1880 produced a distinct and identifiable body of flute literature representative of the Napoleonic age in France and also the Romantic period as a whole....The literature of the French flute school represents a hybrid form of instrumental virtuosity and extremely expressive melodies which holds a unique place in flute literature. Nevertheless its use appears to be decreasing steadily, probably due to differing opinion about the questionable musical value of this body of music. The present study was therefore devised to identify idiosyncratic characteristics of the literature, and to examine possible pedagogical applications in light of these characteristics.... Biographical information was included to enlarge the sociological picture of the flutists' status as Romantic virtuosi, and to aid in the presentation of various descriptions of the expressive role of the new flute. One composition by each composer was selected for analysis. Where possible, actual Conservatory Exam pieces were chosen. A pool of recurrent common characteristics emerged which are clearly related to the sociological framework of nineteenth-century France. Finally, the isolated elements were examined for possible pedagogical benefits.

Jacobus chose Andersen's *Concertstück*, op. 3, and studied aspects of melody, form, rhythm, gestures, dynamics, and style, then compared the composition to pieces by the other five composers.

B25

Priore, Irna Fernanda. "The Flute and Piano Repertoire of Joachim Andersen: A Pedagogical Approach." D. M. diss., City University of New York, 1993.

Dissertation designed to "revive interest in [Joachim Andersen's solo pieces], not only because they are important samples of nineteenth-century flute music, but because they can also serve as a powerful tool in flute pedagogy." The document contains a biography of Andersen, a general comparison of the eight-keyed flute and the Boehm flute, and a catalogue (with brief remarks) of Andersen's compositions. Priore divides Andersen's flute and piano pieces into three categories according to level of difficulty, then analyzes one work in each category. While this author disagrees with some of the material presented in the biography, the project does provide a catalogue of Andersen's flute and piano compositions which could be helpful in reviving interest in these neglected pieces.

Secondary Sources

General Biographies

B26

Abrahamsen, Erik. *Dansk Biografisk Leksikon.* Edited by Svend Cedergreen
Bech. Copenhagen: Gyldendal, 1979-1984. S.v. "Andersen, Carl Joachim."

Well-known, standard Danish encyclopedia offering an accurate and
comparatively complete biography of Joachim Andersen with a short, valuable
bibliography. Mention is made of all of Andersen's major professional
positions as well as his work as a composer. Because the article was not updated
for the 1984 edition, some details are no longer correct. (His urn cannot be found
at Bispebjerg cemetery, and neither the bust made by Sophie Claudius nor the set
of wooden engravings is now in Tivoli Gardens.)

B27

Adams, Carl. "Joachim Andersen: His Compositions for the Flute." *The
Flutist Quarterly* 12, no. 4 (Spring 1987): 71-75.

Short article containing a biographical sketch, a list of Andersen's eight standard
etude books with the etudes' keys, their arrangement in each volume and then-
current publication information, and a list of available works for flute and piano.

B28

Aumont, Arthur. *Salmonsens Konversations Leksikon,* 2nd ed. Edited by Chr.
Blangstrup. Copenhagen: J. H. Schultz, 1923. S.v. "Casino."

Standard Danish encyclopedia. The "Casino" article provides general background
information about the history of the theater where Andersen performed recitals
during the early years of his career. See Biography, p. 2.

B29

Bailey, John. "The Elusive Mr. Andersen." *Flute Talk* 1, no. 9 (May 1982): 1.

One-page article articulating the paradox that every flute student practices
Andersen's etudes, yet few know anything about the composer in spite of his
renown in the nineteenth century. The article, part of an issue of *Flute Talk*
devoted to Andersen, includes standard biographical information and mentions a
number of Andersen's flute compositions.

B30

Basso, Alberto, ed. *Dizionario Enciclopedico Universale Della Musica E Dei Musicisti. Le Biografie.* Torino: Unione Tipografico, 1985. S.v. "Andersen, Karl Joachim."

Encyclopedia article presenting a chronology of Andersen's career with an incomplete list of compositions and related information about Christian Joachim and Vigo Andersen. While the article is brief, its presence attests to Andersen's influence outside Denmark and Germany.

B31

Bate, Philip. *The New Grove Dictionary of Music and Musicians.* Edited by Stanley Sadie. London: Macmillan, 1980. S.v. "Andersen, Karl Joachim."

One-paragraph biographical sketch highlighting major events in Andersen's career. While this article mentions "48 flute studies," it does not emphasize Andersen's legacy as the foremost composer of flute etudes. The characteristically strong Grove bibliography is absent from the entry.

B32

Christiansen, Toke Lund. Liner notes for *Morceaux pour la Flûte avec accompagnement de Piano par Joachim Andersen.* SteepleChase Productions, No. 32079, 1991.

Two-page article highlighting major events in Joachim Andersen's life and career. Toke Lund Christiansen, currently Denmark's leading flutist (Principal flutist of the Danish National Radio Orchestra and flute professor at the Danish Royal Conservatory of Music), also includes general historical information and an anecdote related by Marcel Moyse regarding Andersen's visit to the Paris Conservatory in 1904. See Biography, p. 14.

B33

Dzapo, Kyle. "The Life and Musical Contributions of Joachim Andersen." *The Flutist Quarterly* 21, no. 1 (Fall 1995): 72-76.

Biographical article abstracted from the author's Doctor of Music thesis listed above. (B22) Photographs of Joachim and Vigo Andersen are included. The article offered the most detailed biography of Andersen at the time of its publication, but additional recent research makes the present publication more complete and accurate. The author has now located marriage records for Andersen's parents, birth records for Andersen and his siblings, divorce records for Andersen (which show that Ernst was Joachim's and Emma's natural child and not an adopted child, as had been reported in "Victor Gandrup's Collection about Joachim Andersen" (B7), Berlin "Philharmonic Concert" performance reviews, extensive information about the early years of the Berlin Philharmonic Orchestra (revealing that the fire which probably destroyed manuscripts of Andersen's compositions occurred not at his home, but at the Scheveningen spa where the orchestra performed), newspaper articles which augment understanding of the final years of Andersen's professional life in Copenhagen, and other archival information.

B34

Ljungar-Chapelon, Anders. Introduction to *98 Posthumous Exercises & Preludes*, by Joachim Andersen. C. 1879-1909. Facsimile edition, Stockholm: Autographus Musicus, 1989.

One-page introduction to a long-forgotten collection of etudes. Ljungar-Chapelon relates helpful biographical information, including a valuable paragraph about Christian Joachim Andersen, Joachim's father. A chronology of Andersen's professional activities, miscellaneous information about the etudes, and a brief bibliography are also included.

B35

Magnussen, Julius, ed. *Danske Komponister i Vore Dage*. Copenhagen: Gjellerup, 1901. S.v. "Andersen, Joachim."

One-and-a-half-page general biography of Andersen's professional career in a source titled, "Danish Composers in Our Day." The article is less detailed than Erik Abrahamsen's article in the *Dansk Biografisk Leksikon*. (B26)

B36

Priore, Irna. Preface to *The Andersen Collection*. Valley Forge, Pennsylvania: European American Music Corporation, 1994.

One-page biographical introduction to this recently published collection of Andersen compositions, extracted from the author's dissertation, "The Flute and Piano Repertoire of Joachim Andersen: A Pedagogical Approach." (B25)

B37

Riemann, Hugo, ed. *Musik-Lexikon*. Berlin: Max Hesses, 1929. S.v. "Andersen, Karl Joachim."

Brief biographical article similar to Andersen articles in other encyclopedias.

B38
Schiørring, Nils. *Die Musik in Geschichte und Gegenwart.* Edited by Friedrich
    Blume. Kassel: Barenreiter, 1949-79. S.v. "Andersen, Carl Joachim."

Brief biographical article outlining the major events in Andersen's professional
life, similar in length and content to the Grove article (B31), but including a
short bibliography.

Flute-Related Sources

B39
De Lorenzo, Leonardo. *My Complete Story of the Flute.* 2d ed., rev. and exp.
    Lubbock, Texas: Texas Tech University Press, 1992.

Personal account of the flute and flutists in Europe and America during the mid-
twentieth century. Divided into four parts, the book begins with "The Flute,"
which offers a history of the instrument followed by a description of instruments
in the flute family. Part Two, "The Performer," presents biographies of flute
"pioneers," including an incomplete Andersen biography, then shorter
"thumbnail" sketches of hundreds of flutists, including Christian Joachim
Andersen (Joachim's father), Joachim, and Vigo Andersen (Joachim's brother).
Joachim is also mentioned as the teacher of Ary van Leeuwen and Jay Plow
(*sic*). Because many of Andersen's contemporaries are included, this section is
valuable for identifying his lesser known colleagues. Some pictures and portraits
are included, but none of the Andersens. Part Three, "A Thing or Two about
Flute Music," provides miscellaneous notes about repertoire and composers
(with no mention of Andersen's compositions), and Part Four includes
"Reminiscences of a Flutist." Most notable and often quoted is De Lorenzo's
account of the reason for Andersen's tongue paralysis. See Biography, p. 11.

B40
Fairley, Andrew. *Flutes, Flautists & Makers.* London: Pan Educational Music,
    1982.

Brief biographical sketches of active flutists and those born before 1900. Pages
four and five provide biographies and photographs of Christian Joachim
Andersen (Joachim's father) and Vigo Andersen (Joachim's brother), as well as a
drawing of Joachim. Christian Joachim's biography is the only source which

mentions that he wrote several small works for flute and piano which are charming in character. Joachim's biography states that he was chamber musician to the Russian, Prussian, and Danish courts. Many pictures of historic flutes are included, but no information is provided about Andersen's eight-keyed instrument.

B41

Finn, John. "Flutes and Flute Music." *Musical Opinion* 247 (April 1, 1898): 451.

List of Andersen's compositions with opus numbers and publishers of first editions, omitting the piano compositions (which were written after publication of the article). The author writes that the works published by Max Leichssenring of Hamburg are "now" issued by Ruhle & Hunger of Berlin.

B42

Goldberg, A. *Biographien zur Porträts-Sammlung hervorragender Flöten-Virtuosen, Dilettanten und Komponisten.* 2 vols. Berlin: Meisenbach, Riffarth & Co., 1906.

Collection of biographies and portraits of "the most meaningful masters of the flute, and virtuosi and amateurs of the present." Pages fifteen through eighteen provide a one-page biography of Christian Joachim, a two-page biography of Joachim, and a very brief biography of Vigo.

B43

Hamilton, Amy. "Getting the Most out of Practicing Andersen Etudes." *Flute Talk* 1, no. 9 (May 1982): 2-3.

General guide for effective study of etudes. Hamilton, noting that Andersen's etudes are not only technically challenging but also musically enjoyable, suggests ideas for mastering the technical demands, then, citing op. 33, no. 5, as an example, highlights the structural melody which provides the etude's musical interest.

B44

Kujala, Walfrid. "Andersen's *Scherzino.*" *Flute Talk* 1, no. 9 (May 1982): 5-7.

Instructional guide for performance of Andersen's op. 55, no. 6. Identifying the popular "Scherzino" as an ideal encore piece, Kujala writes an article addressing "performance conventions that are not readily apparent from the notation" (primarily regarding note lengths and rubato). A copy of the flute part is included on pages six and seven with editorial markings by the author.   The markings provide suggestions for tempo, alternate fingerings, specific places for the implementation of rubato, and effective breathing with precise rhythm.

B45
Nyfenger, Thomas. *Music and the Flute*. Privately published, 1989.

Valuable pedagogical book written by the long-time flute professor at Yale University. In a section titled, "Etudes Forever," Nyfenger expresses his point of view regarding the value of etudes, provides a general guide for effective and efficient practice of etudes, then writes practice suggestions for each of the twenty-four exercises in Andersen's op. 15 collection. It is noteworthy that Nyfenger chose this etude book.

B46
Randalls, Jeremy. "Andersen's Expression Marks: The 24 Etudes, op. 15." *The Flutist Quarterly* 22, no. 3 (Spring 1997): 30-31.

Article containing translations of the often obscure stylistic markings used by Andersen in his opus 15 collection of etudes.

B47
Rockstro, Richard Shepard. *A Treatise on the Construction the History and the Practice of the Flute*. 1890, 2nd ed., rev. 1928. Reprint, London: Music Rara, 1967.

Well-known flute treatise aptly described by its title.   Ironically, several sources list this book in their Andersen bibliographies, though he is mentioned only on pages 518 and 519, where four of his compositions (op. 2, 24, 22, and 23) are listed without elaboration.

B48
Toff, Nancy. *The Flute Book*. 2nd ed. New York: Oxford University Press, 1996.

Guide for flute students and performers with sections on the instrument (history, care and maintenance, models and features, etc.), performance technique (breathing, tone, vibrato, articulation, technique, etc.), and repertoire of each style period from Baroque to twentieth century. A list of currently published compositions includes a number of Andersen works. Toff also cites him as the model of flute playing in Denmark and Germany during the nineteenth century and notes that Paul Taffanel commissioned him to write the 1895 *concours* piece for the Paris Conservatory.

History of the Berlin Philharmonic Orchestra

B49

Altmann, Wilhelm. *Chronik des Berliner Philharmonischen Orchesters (1882-1901)*. Berlin: Schuster & Loeffler, 1902.

One of the first books to recount the early history of the Berlin Philharmonic Orchestra. The book includes information about the initial successes and travails of the orchestra, the "Philharmonic Society" which was formed in 1884 to boost financial support for the orchestra, and "Paris tuning," adopted during the early years of the Philharmonic, which required the purchase of new wind instruments in 1885.   (These instruments and other belongings were destroyed in a devastating fire at the orchestra's summer home in Scheveningen, Holland, September 1, 1886.)

B50

Avgerinos, Gerassimos.   *Das Berliner Philharmonische Orchester als eigenständige Organisation: 70 Jahre Schicksal einer GMBH 1882-1952*. Berlin: Privately published, 1972.

Publication honoring the seventieth anniversary of the Berlin Philharmonic Orchestra.   The book consists of a sixty-seven-page history of the orchestra followed by chapters devoted to the Pension Fund, Widows and Orphans Fund, Women's Guild, and Membership Club.   A list of Orchestra Committee members, executive directors with brief biographies, and conductors is included. The bibliography is the same as Avgerinos' *Künstler-Biographien: Die Mitglieder im Berliner Philharmonischen Orchester von 1882-1972*. (B51)

B51

Avgerinos, Gerassimos. *Künstler-Biographien: Die Mitglieder im Berliner Philharmonischen Orchester von 1882-1972*. Berlin: Privately published, 1971.

Book written to commemorate the ninetieth anniversary of the Berlin Philharmonic Orchestra. It contains short biographies of past and present members of the orchestra, including a one-page general biography of Andersen. Also included are lists of concertmasters, principal cellists, members who conducted the Berlin Philharmonic or who became conductors (including Andersen), members who composed (including Andersen), authors, members who wrote arrangements, method books and etudes (including Andersen), and administrators. Avgerinos includes a good bibliography of materials related to the history of the orchestra.

B52
Badde, Paul, Ulrich Borsdorf, et al. *Das Berliner Philharmonische Orchester.*
    Stuttgart: Deutsche Verlags-Anstalt, 1987.

Ten-page history of the Berlin Philharmonic Orchestra written by Peter Cossé, followed by essays about various aspects of orchestral music-making in recent years (Behind the Scenes, Leisure Time, Media, Touring, etc.), concluding with a timeline of the history of the orchestra by Jutta March.

B53
Einstein, Alfred. *Fünfzig Jahre Philharmonisches Orchester*, with an essay,
    "Das Philharmonische Orchester," by Wilhelm Furtwängler. 1932.

Brief history of the first fifty years of the Berlin Philharmonic Orchestra. Einstein describes the years during which Andersen was a member of the orchestra, mentioning him when listing the program of the Philharmonic's first concert on October 17, 1882.

B54
Herzfeld, Friedrich. *Berliner Philharmonisches Orchester 1882-1942.*   Berlin:
    Berlin Philharmonic Orchestra, 1942.

Book commissioned by the Berlin Philharmonic Orchestra to commemorate the sixtieth anniversary of the orchestra. This short book has three essays: "How It Began" by Fred Hamel, "A Treasury of German Music Culture" by Heinz Joachim, and "The Berlin Philharmonic in the Years 1922-1942" by Friedrich Herzfeld. The general history does not mention Andersen.

B55
Muck, Peter. *Einhundert Jahre Berliner Philharmonisches Orchester.*   3 vols.
    Tutzing: Hans Schneider, 1982.

Large three-volume work, written for the one hundredth anniversary of the founding of the Berlin Philharmonic. This source offers the most complete and detailed information regarding the history of the orchestra.

Volume one traces the orchestra's history from 1882 to 1922. The first three chapters (Founding - 1882-84; Three Years of the Society, 1884-87; and von Bülow 1887-92) provide 170 pages of material about the years during which Andersen was a member of the orchestra.

Volume two traces the orchestra's history from 1922-1982.

Volume three includes a list of orchestra members, past and present, organized by instrument; lists of executive directors and stage managers; a list of concert programs, including works performed with other organizations and works performed on tours; a list of premieres (world premieres, first performances in Berlin, and first performances by the Berlin Philharmonic Orchestra) and a list of soloists (including speakers, dancers, and conductors), with date of first performance with the orchestra.

The three volumes are illustrated and include portraits of significant people involved with the orchestra, pictures of the orchestra, agreements signed, correspondence, newspaper articles, and other pertinent documents.

B56

Oehlmann, Werner. *Das Berliner Philharmonische Orchester.* Kassel: Barenreiter, 1974.

Two chapters (I. Founding and Early Years and II. Hans von Bülow) provide pertinent information about the Berlin Philharmonic during Andersen's tenure. Andersen is cited on page seventeen as "the first who should be mentioned among the wind players," noting that he was a virtuoso master of the flute and later a conductor in Berlin and Copenhagen. Page twenty lists the program of the first popular concert in October of 1882 when Andersen performed Ciardi's *Le Carnaval Russe*. The book also contains a timeline of important events occurring between May 1, 1882, and July 1, 1973.

B57

Stargardt-Wolff, Edith. *Wegbereiter grosser Musiker.* Berlin: Bote & G. Bock, 1954.

Detailed description of Berlin's concert life in the late nineteenth century as recounted by the daughter of Berlin's leading impresario, Hermann Wolff. Wolff, a concert agent hired by the Berlin Philharmonic Orchestra in 1882 to advise and promote the ensemble, shaped much that occurred during the early years of the orchestra. In "Path Breaker for Great Musicians," Edith Stargardt-Wolff provides an intimate, adulatory look at her father's professional life, including a chapter on Berlin's emergence as a center of music in the 1880s and a chapter on conductor Hans von Bülow. Hermann Wolff worked closely with von Bülow during his tenure as conductor of the orchestra and much of their correspondence is published in the book.

B58
Stresemann, Wolfgang.   *The Berlin Philharmonic from Bülow to Karajan.*
   Translated by Jean Stresemann. Berlin: Stapp, 1979.

Most complete history of the Berlin Philharmonic Orchestra in English.   The book provides a well-written account of the Bilse Orchestra, the development and early years of the Berlin Philharmonic and the von Bülow years, continuing through the von Karajan years. There is no mention of Andersen.

B59
Weissmann, Adolf.   *Berlin als Musikstadt: Geschichte der Oper und des Konzerts von 1740 bis 1911.* Berlin: Schuster & Loeffler, 1911.

Detailed account of the early years of the Berlin Philharmonic Orchestra.   The book describes concert life in Berlin during the years of the Bilse Orchestra, tells of the electrifying Meiningen Orchestra concert in 1882, then chronicles events during the Philharmonic's first years. Weissmann includes information about the Philharmonic's popular concerts and conductors Kogel, Brenner, and Mannstädt, but Andersen is not mentioned.

Copenhagen During Andersen's Lifetime

B60
Clausen, Julius. *Mennesker paa min vej.* Copenhagen: Gyldendal, 1941.

Personal account ("People Along My Way"), written by a Danish author and librarian.   The book contains information about Danish theater, poets and writers, the Royal Library, universities, and music, including a brief description of Andersen's work as conductor of the Tivoli Orchestra. From Clausen, the reader learns about Andersen's discipline of the orchestra and his shortcomings when conducting compositions new to him.

B61

Fabricius, Lars Børge. *Træk Af Dansk Musiklivs Historie M. M.* Copenhagen: Arnold Busck, 1975.

Book containing information about Danish musical life during composer Jacob Christian Fabricius' life (1840-1919), including several pages about the early years of Andersen's Palace Concerts. See Biography, p. 17.

B62

Fischer, Wilhelm, ed. *Orkesterforeningens Medlemsblad.* Copenhagen: Nielsen, 1909. S. v. "Andersen, Joachim."

Monthly journal for Danish orchestra union members. Two articles in 1909 contain announcements about Andersen. The first congratulates him on his appointment as "Professor of Music." The second reports his death. A large portion of the obituary is quoted on page 31 of the Biography.

B63

Friis, Niels. *Det Kongelige Kapel.* Copenhagen: Haase & Sons, 1948.

Comprehensive history of the Danish Royal Orchestra between 1448 and 1948, subtitled, "Five Centuries at Court, in the Theatre and in Concert Halls." Among the most highly regarded orchestras in Scandinavia, the Royal Orchestra employed the finest musicians in Denmark. Joachim and Vigo Andersen were both members of the orchestra during the early years of their careers and are briefly mentioned by Friis. The book includes complete personnel lists for members of the orchestra between 1770 and 1948, with instrument played and dates of service.

B64

Hansen, Anton. *En Kgl. Kapelmusikers Erindringer.* Collected and edited by Per Gade. Copenhagen: Quality Music Press, 1996.

Memoirs of Anton Hansen (1877-1947), a trombonist and member of the Palace and Tivoli orchestras during Andersen's tenure as conductor. Hansen was also a member of the Royal Orchestra between 1905 and 1942. The book includes information about the early years of the Palace Concerts, the development of the Rosenborg concerts, and anecdotes about Andersen's conducting style and personality. Much of the material duplicates information contained in Nils Schiørring's *Fund og Forskning* articles. (B68 and B69)

B65

Harvild, G. K. *Tivoli Past and Present.* Copenhagen: Tivoli Gardens, 1927.

Source in English detailing the history and development of Tivoli Gardens, Copenhagen's world-renowned entertainment center. After introducing founder Georg Carstensen's concept for the Gardens, the illustrated guide provides pictures and descriptions of the main attractions in the park at the time of publication. Included is the Glass Hall, the concert hall where the Tivoli Orchestra performed from its inception until 1902 when a new hall was built.

B66

Mentze, Ernst and Harald H. Lund, ed. *Tivoli Minder.* Copenhagen: Carl Allers, 1943.

Commemorative book written to celebrate the one hundredth anniversary of Tivoli Gardens. The book contains forty pages of information and pictures about the music of Tivoli. Written by Aage Bruun, this section provides information about Andersen's elegant appearance, his strict discipline of the orchestra, the opening of the new concert hall in 1902, and his idea to ask the audience to choose performance pieces. Also included are a picture of the orchestra in 1863 when Joachim's father was a member, a portrait of Andersen, and a picture of Andersen with his orchestra during the summer 1900 season.

B67

Neiiendam, Robert. *Casino. Oprindelse og Historie i Omrids.* Copenhagen: M. A. Korch, 1923.

Commemorative book written to celebrate the one hundredth anniversary of the Casino Theater. Though it does not mention Andersen, this source provides background information about the history of the hall where he and his brother performed numerous recitals.

B68

Schiørring, Niels, ed. "Fra Tivoligarden til Det Kongelige Kapel Uddrag af Anton Hansens Erindringer I," *Fund og Forskning* 14 (1967): 103-158.

Lengthy article, "From the Tivoli Guard to the Royal Orchestra: The Memoirs of Anton Hansen, I," recounting stories of trombonist Anton Hansen's childhood and professional life. Hansen, a musician in Andersen's Palace and Tivoli orchestras as well as a member of the Royal Orchestra, relates numerous anecdotes about Andersen's personality and conducting style. This article predates Hansen's *En Kgl. Kapelmusikers Erindringer* (B64), which includes much of the same information concerning Andersen.

B69
Schiørring, Niels, ed. "Af Anton Hansens Erindringer II," *Fund og Forskning* 15 (1968): 117-159.

Continuation of the preceding article. This account tells of Danish musical life during the period 1890 to 1930 and presents Anton Hansen's reminiscences and opinions about a number of eminent musicians he came to know. Among them are conductors under whose baton he played, including Johan Svendsen, Carl Nielsen, Joachim Andersen, and Franz Schnedler-Petersen, the latter two receiving special mention.

B70
Schnedler-Petersen, Franz. *Et Liv i Musik.* Copenhagen: Novografia, 1946.

Memoirs of Franz Schnedler-Petersen, Andersen's successor as conductor of both the Palace Concerts and the Tivoli Orchestra. The book, arranged chronologically, tells of Schnedler-Petersen's work as a violinist (including both orchestral and solo performances), his year as interim conductor of the Tivoli Orchestra in 1897, and his work after Andersen's death. A lengthy index of works first performed in Tivoli during Schnedler-Petersen's thirty-five years as conductor (1909-34) includes a citation for Andersen's *Fantaisie Caractéristique*, op. 16, performed July 19, 1911.

Appendix 1

Representative Programs of Concerts in which Joachim Andersen Participated as Flutist or Conductor

2^{den}

Soirée for Kammermusik
I CASINOS MINDRE SAL
af Medlemmer af det kongl. Capel.

----

1. **L. van Beethoven**, op. 24, Sonate i F, for Piano og Violin.
   Allegro.
   Adagio.
   Scherzo.
   Rondo.
   D'Herr. **Victor Bendix** og **Hilmer**.

2. **R. Schumann**, op. 42, "Frauenliebe und Leben," Sang-Cyclus.
   Frk. C. Pfeil.

3. **J. Raff**, op. 188, Sinfonietta i F, for 2 Fløiter, 2 Oboer, 2 Clarinetter,
   2 Fagotter og 2 Horn.
   Allegro.
   Allegro molto.
   Larghetto.
   Vivace.

   D'Herr. **Jørgen Petersen, Joachim Andersen, Schiemann, Otto
   Bendix, C. Stockmar, Mathiesen, V. Andersen,
   Guldbrandsen, Joh. Petersen** og **Dreves**.

Forbi omtrent Kl. 9.

1875-76

Example 1.   Chamber music concert, Casino Theater, Copenhagen, 1875-76
season. Andersen performed in numerous chamber music concerts at
the Casino during his tenure as flutist with the Royal Orchestra.

4^{de}
Soirée for Kammermusik
I CASINOS MINDRE SAL
af Medlemmer af det kongl. Capel.

----

1. **W. A. Mozart**, Divertimento for Violin, Viola og Violoncel.
    Allegro.
    Adagio.
    Menuetto: Allegretto.
    Andante con Variazioni.
    Menuetto: Allegretto.
    Allegro.
    D-Hrr. Anton Svendsen, Holm og Rydinger.

2. **P. Heise**, Sange.
    Frk. Augusta Schou.

3. **L. Spohr**, op. 147, Septet i a moll for Piano, Violin, Violoncel, Fløite,
    Clarinet, Horn og Fagot.
    Allegro vivace.
    Larghetto pastorale.
    Scherzo: vivace.
    Finale: molto allegro.

    D'Hrr.   Otto Bendix, Schjørring, Fritz Bendix, J. Andersen, C. Stockmar,
             Joh. Petersen og V. Andersen.

Forbi omtrent Kl. 9 1/4

1876-77

Example 2.   Chamber music concert, Casino Theater, Copenhagen, 1876-77
season. Andersen performed in numerous chamber music concerts at
the Casino during his tenure as flutist with the Royal Orchestra.

Philharmonie
Bernburger - Strasse 22a.

Heute
1. CONCERT
des Philharmonischen Orchesters
unter Leitung seines Dirigenten des Königlichen Musikdirectors
Herrn **Professor von Brenner**.

PROGRAMM.

I. Theil
1.	Ouverture zu Leonore III	L. v. Beethoven.
2.	Andante cantabile, Streichquartett	Tschaikowsky.
	Vorgetr. v. d. g sammten Streichquartett.	
3.	Non piu mesta, Variationen f. Violine	Paganini.
	Vorgetr. v. Concertmeister Hrn. Prof. Thomson.	
4.	Vorspiel z. Op. "Die Meistersinger von Nürnberg"	Wagner.

II. Theil
5.	Z. 1. Mal. Ouvert. z. Op. 'König Manfred'	Reinecke.
6.	Le carnaval russe, Fantasie f. Flöte	Ciardi.
	Vorgetr. v. Hrn. Joachim Andersen.	
7.	Nocturno f. Cello m. Harfenbegleitung	Chopin.
	Vorgetr. v. Hrn. Antoine Hekking. (Harfe: Hr. Müller)	
8.	Z. 1. Mal. Slavische Rhapsodie No. II	Dvorak.

III. Theil.
9.	Ouverture z. Op. "Wilhelm Tell"	Rossini.
10.	Z. 1. Mal Schwedischer Tanz f. Streichorchester	Gouvy.
11.	Polonaise No. II in E	Liszt.
	Orchestrirt v. Müller-Berghaus.	

Anfang 7 Uhr.   Ende 10 Uhr.

Example 3.   Inaugural concert of the Berlin Philharmonic Orchestra, October 17, 1882.   Joachim Andersen, principal flutist of the ensemble, performed as a soloist on this concert.

Kurhaus de Schéveningue.

Samedi 23 Août 1890.
CONCERTS de l'Orchestre Philharmonique de Berlin.
PROGRAMMES:

de 3 à 4 heures 1/2 de l'après-midi.
sous la direction de M^r. JOACHIM ANDERSEN.

1. Ouverture zu "Stradella"	F. v. Flotow.
2. Valse pour Instruments à cordes	P. Tschaikowsky.
3. Pesther-Walzer	Jos. Lanner.

---

4. Ouverture zu "Jessonda"	L. Spohr.
5. Variationen A-dur für Streichquartett	L. v. Beethoven.
6. Roxana, Marsch	L. Mincauis.

à 7 heures 1/2 du soir,
sous la direction du Chef d'Orchestre M^r. GUSTAV KOGEL.

1. Marche héroïque	C. Saint-Saëns
2. "Zur Weihe des Hauses" Ouverture	L. v. Beethoven.
3.* Andante aus dem Streichquartett, Op. 11	P. Tschaikowsky.
4. Fantasie über Motive aus Wagner's "Lohengrin"	A. Dupont.

---

5. Ouverture de "Guillaume Tell"	G. Rossini.
6.* a. Andante für Flöte	B. Molique.
b. Valse für Flöte mit Harfenbegleitung	Chopin-Taffanel.
(Herr Otto Müller)	
Vorgetragen von Herrn Joachim Andersen.	
7. Nocturne und Scherzo aus "Ein Sommernachtstraum"	F. Mendelssohn.
8.* Gavotte pour Instruments à cordes	E. Gillet.
9. Anderschönen blauen Donau, Walzer	J. Strauss.

Example 4.   Summer concerts of the Berlin Philharmonic Orchestra, presented at the Orchestra's summer home in Scheveningen, Holland, August 23, 1890.   Andersen conducted the 3:00 p.m. concert and performed Bernhard Molique's "Andante" and an arrangement of a Chopin waltz on the evening concert.

Kurhaus de Schéveningue.

Vendredi 19 Septembre 1890.
CONCERTS de l'Orchestre Philharmonique de Berlin.
PROGRAMMES:
de 3 à 4 heures 1/2 de l'après-midi,
sous la direction de M^r. JOACHIM ANDERSEN.

1. Priestermarsch aus "Athalia"   F. Mendelssohn.
2. Ouverture des "Deux Journées" ("Der Wasserträger")   L. Cherubini.
3. Du und Du, Walzer   Joh. Strauss.

———————

4. Ouverture de "La Muette de Portici"   D. F. E. Auber.
5. a. Abendlied   Rob. Schumann.
   b. Loin du bal   E. Gillet.
6. Türkischer Marsch aus "Die Ruinen von Athen"   L. v. Beethoven.

———————

A 7 heures 1/2 du soir,
sous la direction du Chef d'Orchestre M^r. GUSTAV KOGEL.

QUATORZIÈME CONCERT SYMPHONIQUE.

1. Ouverture zu Shakespeare's Drama "Hamlet"   Niels W. Gade.
2. Largo Arioso (*Auf Wunsch*)   G. F. Händel.
                Violine-Solo: Herr Concertmeister L. Bleuer.
3. SINFONIE N°5 C-moll   L. v. Beethoven.
   a. Allegro con brio; b. Andante con moto; c. Scherzo und Finale.

———————

4. Ouverture solennelle (1812)   P. Tschaikowsky.
5. PIRUN POLSKA. Finnisches Tanzlied.   Joachim Andersen.
   für Flöte und Orchester.
                Vorgetragen von Componisten.
6. Danse macabre, Poème Symphonique   C. Saint-Saëns.
7. DEUX RHAPSODIES SCANDINAVES   E. Lalo.
   a. La majeur; b. Ré mineur.

Example 5.   Summer concerts of the Berlin Philharmonic Orchestra, presented at
the Orchestra's summer home in Scheveningen, Holland, September
19, 1890.   Andersen conducted the 3:00 p.m. concert and performed
his *Pirun Polska* for flute and orchestra, op. 49, on the evening
concert.

V. **Palæ-Koncert**   { Onsdag d. 11. Novbr. 1896 Aften Kl. 8.
                          { Søndag d. 15.   ---   ---   Eftm. - 4 1/2.

PROGRAM:
1. Rob. Volkmann: **Ouverture** til Shakespeares Drama **"Richard den III."**
2. L. v. Beethoven: **Balletmusik af "Prometheus"** (1ste Opførelse)
   Soli: Violoncello: Hr. **Eiler Jensen**.
              Harpe: Frk. **M. Heyn**.
              Fløjte: Hr. **Leo Lottenburger**.
              Clarinet: Hr. **C. Skjerne**.
              Fagot: Hr. **Devald**.
3. C. F. E. Horneman: **Musik** til Paludan-Müllers **"Kalanus."**
   a. **Forspil**.   }
   b. **Intermezzo**.   } (1ste Opførelse.)
   c. **Kalanus Drøm**.   }
   d. **Indledning** til Ill. Akt.   }
4. R. Würst: a. **"Träumerai"** af den russiske Suite.
             (**Violinsolo**: Hr. **F. Schnedler-Petersen**.)
          b. **Unterm Balkon**.
             Violoncelsolo: Hr. Eiler Jensen.
5. Weber-Berlioz: **Invitation à la Valse**.

IX. **Palæ-Koncert**   { Onsdag d. 13. Januar 1897, Aften Kl. 8.
                          { Søndag d. 17.   ---   ---   Eftm. - 4 1/2.

PROGRAM:

1. Carl Nielsen: **Symphoni** i G-moll.
2. Händel: **Largo arioso**.
   Soli: Engelsk Horn: Hr. **P. Brøndum**.
              Harpe: Frøken **M. Heyn**.
              Orgel: Hr. Professor **J. H. Nebelong**.
3. Anton Rubinstein: **Koncert** i D-moll for **Klaver** og **Orkester**.
              Klaver: Hr. Hofpianist **Georg Liebling**.
4. Aug. Enna: **Fragmenter** af **"Aucassin og Nicolete"**
5. A. Dvorák: **To slaviske Danse** (1ste Opførelse).

Example 6. Palace Concerts, Copenhagen, November 11 and 15, 1896, and
            January 13 and 17, 1897. Andersen served as Music Director of the
            Palace Concerts between 1894 and 1909 and conducted both of these
            performances.

København   14de Sæson 1908 - 1909

Søndag d. 28. Marts 1909 Kl. 4 Eftm.

19de Palæ-Koncert.
(304. Palæ-Koncert)
Næstsidste   Koncert.

Direktion: **JOACHIM ANDERSEN**

Medvirkning:
Frøken **Karen Oderwald-Lander** (Sang).

PROGRAM.

1. FR. SCHUBERT: **H-moll Symfoni.** (Den ufuldendte).
   Allegro moderato.
   Andante con moto.

2. AMBR. THOMAS: **Polonaise** af Op. **"Mignon"**
   Synges af Frøken **Karen Oderwald-Lander**.

3. C. SAINT-SAËNS: a. **Forspil** til det bibelske Oratorium **"Syndfloden."**
   b. **Præstindernes Dans** af Op. **"Samson og Dalila."**

4. P. RODE: **Thema med Variationer** for Sopran.
   Synges af Frøken **Karen Oderwald-Lander**.

5. RICHARD WAGNER: **Smedjesange** af Musikdramaet **"Siegfred."**

Tekst: Se 4 Side.

Example 7. Palace Concert, Copenhagen, March 28, 1909. This was the final Palace Concert program conducted by Andersen. Following the concert, he met with the orchestral musicians and announced his retirement due to illness. Andersen died on May 9, 1909. (His second wife, Sarah Dana Watson Andersen, wrote "the last" on this program, then donated it and other materials to the New York Public Library for the Performing Arts.)

Joachim Andersens Orkester-Skole

i Forbindelse med

Det kgl. danske Musik-Konservatoriums Orkesterelever.

16de Skole=Matinée

(12. Skolcaar)

for indbudt Publikum

Odd Fellow-Palæets store Sal,

Mandag d. 20 April 1908 (2^den Paaskedag) Kl. 12 prc

Med velvillig Assistance af Fagmusikere, der komplettere Skole-Orkestret

Direktion: Joachim Andersen.

PROGRAM

1. Joseph Haydn: **Oxford Symfoni.**
   (Nr. 16, G-dur, i *Breitkopf & Härtels* Udgave)
   a. Adagio - Allegro spiritoso.
   b. Adagio.
   c. Menuetto.
   d. Finale. Presto.

2. W. A. Mozart: **Jupiter Symfoni.** (No. 4, C-dur).
   a. Allegro vivace.
   b. Andante cantabile.
   c. Menuetto.
   d. Finale og Slutningsfuga. Allegro molto.

3. F. Mendelssohn: **Italiensk Symfoni.** (Nr. 4, A-dur)
   a. Allegro vivace.
   b. Andante con moto.
   c. Con moto moderato.
   d. Saltarello. Presto.

Til Deltagelse i Joachim Andersens Orkester-skoles 12te Skoleaar (1907-08), indmeldtes der 66 Elever, (10 Damer og 56 Herrer), 39 Violin, 2 Bratsch, 6 Violoncel, 5 Contra-Bas, 3 Fløjte, 2 Obo, 3 Clarinet, 3 Horn og 3 Trompet.

Trykt i Wilhelm Hansens Etabl., Kjøbenhavn.

Example 8. Orchestra School concert, Odd-Fellow Palace, April 20, 1908. Andersen founded the Orchestra School and served as its Music Director between 1896 and 1909.

Nr. 92   1902.
Fredag 8. Aug. 1902.
Næstsidste Feriefest.
Koncertsalen.
Dirigent: JOACHIM ANDERSEN.

Første Afdeling Kl. 7 1/2.

1. Kroningsmarche af Op. "Die Folkunger"	Kretschmer.
2. Forspil af Musiken til Drachmanns "Renaissance"	P. E. Lange-Müller.
3. Hinduernes Dans af Op. "Perlefiskerne"	G. Bizet.
4. a. Dodelinette, Berceuse	Ch. Gounod.
b. Sommerfugledans af Op. "Pharaos Ring"	Fr. Rung.
5. Tscherhessisk Dans	Aug. Södermann.

Anden Afdeling Kl. 9.

6. Ouverture til Op. "Hunyady Laszlo"	Franz Erkel.
7. Valse Intermezzo af Ball. "Naila"	Leo Délibes.
8. Klokke og Gralsscene af "Parsifal"	Rich. Wagner.
9. Allegro militaire, Koncert-Allegro for 2 Solofløjter	
med Orkester	Joachim Andersen.

Solister: Hr. Leo Lottenburger, 1mo Fløjte.
       "   Rob. Enevoldsen, 2da Fløjte.

Tredie Afdeling Kl. 10 1/2.

10. Ouverture til Grippenkerls Drama "Robespierre"	H. Litolff.
11. Träumerei, af den russiske Suite	R. Wüerst.
(Violinsolo: Hr. Koncertmester: F. Hemme).	
12. Harpe og Spilledaase, Intermezzo	Braun.
13. Fantasi over Motiver af Leoncavallos Op. "Bajadser"	Joh. Döbber.
14. Nyt Aarhundrede, nyt Liv, Vals	Ziehrer.
15. Le Rhin, Mazurka	O. Métra.

Example 9.   Tivoli Orchestra, Tivoli Concert Hall, Copenhagen, August 8, 1902. Andersen served as Music Director of the Tivoli Orchestra between 1898 and 1909. On this concert, his *Allegro Militaire*, op. 48, was performed by the orchestra's two flutists accompanied by the ensemble.

Nr. 47.   Lørdag 1. Juli, 1905.
Koncertsalen.
Dirigent: Joachim Andersen.
3die Symfoni-Koncert.
Solofløjtenist ved den k. k. Hof-Opera i Wien
Reserverede Billetter à 50 Ø. (gyldige til 1ste og 2den
Afdeling) faas fra Kl. 6 1/2 i Billetkonforet.

Første Afdeling Kl. 7 1/2.
1. Fest-Ouverture over to thüringske Folkemelodier   Edv. Lassen.
2. Et Æventyr, Orkesterstykke (1ste G.)   Jean Louis Nicode.
3. Fløjtesoli med Klaverledsagelse.
   a. Danksagung Op. 19 (Nr. 4)   Ary van Leeuwen.
   b. Scherzino af Op. 55 (Nr. 6)   Joachim Andersen.
   c. Vals af Suiten Op. 116   Benjamin Godard.
           Solist: Hr. ARY van LEEUWEN.
       Akkompagnement: Hr. Holger Dahl.
4. Gudernes lødtog i Valhalla, af Musikdramaet "Rhinguldet"   Rich. Wagner.

Anden Afdeling Kl. 9.
5. Forspil til den musikalske Idyl "Janie" (1ste Gang)   F. Jacques-Dalcroze.
6. Koncert i G-Dur for Fløjte med Orkester   W. A. Mozart.
   a. Allegro maestoso.
   b. Adagio non troppo.
   c. Rondo. Tempo di Menuetto.
           Solist: Hr. ARY van LEEUWEN.
7. Symfoni i B-Dur (Nr. 12)   Joseph Haydn.
   a. Largo. Allegro vivace.
   b. Adagio.
   c. Menuetto. Allegro.
   d. Finale. Presto.

Tredie Afdeling Kl. 10 1/2
8. Ouverture til Grippenkerls Drama "Maximilian Robespierre"   H. Littolf.
9. Danse macabre, symfonisk Digtning   C. Saint-Saëns.
10. Fantasi over Motiver af Offenbachs Oprt. "Pariserliv"   A. Schrainer.
11. Meditation over det 1ste Præ'udium af Bach   Ch. Gachad.
           Violinsoluen spilles af Hr. Marius Hansen.
12. La Czarino, Mazurka   L. Ganne.

Example 10. Tivoli Orchestra, Tivoli Concert Hall, Copenhagen, July 1, 1905.
        Andersen served as Music Director of the Tivoli Orchestra between
        1898 and 1909. On this concert, Ary van Leeuwen, Andersen's
        former student, performed "Scherzino," op. 55, no. 6, and two other
        compositions.

Appendix 2

Timeline of Events (1816–1944)

Joachim Andersen's Biography	Joachim Andersen's Works

1816   Christian Joachim Andersen born
       Joachim Andersen's father
      Johann Jansson born
       Joachim Andersen's first wife's
       (Emma's) father

1819   Malin Vikström born
       Joachim Andersen's first wife's
       (Emma's) mother

1823   Caroline Frederikke Andkjær born
       Joachim Andersen's mother

1846   Emma Christina Jansson born
       Joachim Andersen's first wife

1847   Joachim Andersen's parents marry
       Joachim Andersen born (April 29)

	Selected Music Events	Selected World Events
1816	Benjamin Bilse born Bilse Orchestra preceded Berlin Philharmonic Orchestra Rossini, *The Barber of Seville* Schubert, Symphony No. 5	The Grand Duke of Saxe-Weimar grants first constitution in German lands
1823	Beethoven, Symphony No. 9 von Weber, *Euryanthe*	United States proclaims Monroe Doctrine
1830	Berlioz, *Symphonie Fantastique*	
1835		H. C. Andersen, *Tales Told for Children*
1836	*Musikforeningen* founded Famous under Gade during the 1850s and 1860s Meyerbeer, *Les Huguenots*	
1838	Berlioz, *Benvenuto Cellini* First public school instruction in music (Boston)	Dickens, *Oliver Twist* Poe, *Fall of the House of Usher* Photography invented
1839	New York Philharmonic Society founded Vienna Philharmonic founded	King Christian VIII begins reign in Denmark
1842	Glinka, *Russlan and Ludmilla*	Hong Kong taken by England
1843		Tivoli Gardens opens Kierkegaard, *Either/Or*
1846	Mendelssohn, *Elijah*	Segregation in South Africa
1847	Niels Gade appointed conductor of Gewandhaus Orchestra	

Andersen   Andersen's Works

1849   Julie Andersen born
        Joachim Andersen's sister

1852   Vigo Andersen born
        Joachim Andersen's brother

1855   Hilma Andersen born
        Joachim Andersen's sister
        Joachim Andersen enters school and
           begins flute lessons
        Sara Dana Watson born
           Joachim Andersen's second wife

1857   Johann Jansson dies
        Joachim Andersen's first wife's
           (Emma's) father

1860   Joachim Andersen performs debut
           recital at Casino Theater

1861   Joachim Andersen confirmed

Music Events	World Events
1848 Casino Theater opens in Copenhagen	King Frederick VII begins reign in Denmark Revolution in Schleswig and Holstein against Denmark Liberal revolutions sweep German states Marx and Engels, *The Communist Manifesto*
1849 Wagner, *Die Kunst und die Revolution*	First Danish Democratic constitution adopted
1852	Melville, *Moby Dick* Stowe, *Uncle Tom's Cabin*
1853 Verdi, *La Traviata, Il Trovatore*	Crimean War begins
1854 Liszt, Sonata in B Minor	Thoreau, *Walden*
1855 Bizet, Symphony No. 1	Robert Browning, *Men and Women* Whitman, *Leaves of Grass*
1857 Hans von Bülow marries Cosima Liszt	Baudelaire, *Les Fleurs du Mal*
1859 Wagner, *Tristan und Isolde*	Darwin, *On the Origin of Species*
1860 Suppé, *Das Pensionat* (first Viennese operetta)	Abraham Lincoln elected 16th President of the United States; South Carolina secedes from the Union in protest
1861 Royal Academy of Music, London, founded	Emancipation of Russian serfs by Czar Alexander II
1862 Ludwig Köchel, *Catalogue of Mozart's Works*	Bismarck appointed Chief Minister of Prussia
1863	King Christian IX begins reign in Denmark

Andersen   Andersen's Works

1864   Christian Andersen (Joachim
        Andersen's father) discharged
        from Danish military musical
        corps

1867   Thora Gunhild Zurzick born
        Joachim Andersen's son's wife

1869   Joachim Andersen wins position
        in Royal Orchestra
        Joachim Andersen marries Emma
        Christina Jansson

1871   Joachim Andersen granted one-year
        leave of absence from Royal
        Orchestra

1872   Ernst Gunner Joachim Andersen born
        Joachim and Emma Andersen's son
        Joachim Andersen and Emma Chris-
        tina Jansson Andersen separate

1874   Emma Christina Jansson Andersen
        requests divorce from Joachim
        Andersen

1877   Joachim Andersen granted second
        one-year leave of absence from
        Royal Orchestra

Music Events	World Events
1864 Bruckner, Symphony No. 0	Second Schleswig-Holstein War (Denmark loses Schleswig-Holstein to Prussia and Austria) Tolstoy, *War and Peace*
1867 Bilse establishes orchestra in Berlin Danish Royal Conservatory opens Johann Strauss, Jr., *On the Beautiful Blue Danube*	Ibsen, *Peer Gynt* Marx, *Das Kapital*, vol. 1
1868 Brahms, *A German Requiem*	Renoir, *The Skaters*
1869 Cosima Liszt von Bülow leaves Hans von Bülow for Wagner Wagner, *Das Rheingold*	Suez Canal opens
1870 Tchaikovsky, *Romeo and Juliet*	Franco-Prussian War begins
1871 Verdi, *Aida*	Wilhelm I, King of Prussia, proclaimed German emperor Barnum, *Greatest Show on Earth*
1872	Monet, *Impression: Sunrise* Whistler, *The Artist's Mother*
1874 Mussorgsky, *Boris Godunov, Pictures at an Exhibition* Johann Strauss, Jr., *Die Fledermaus*	Degas, *Ballet Rehearsal*
1875 Bizet, *Carmen*	
1876 Bayreuth *Festspielhaus* opens with first performance of *The Ring of the Nibelung*	Telephone invented Mallarmé, *L'après-midi d'un faune* Twain, *Tom Sawyer*
1877 Brahms, Symphony No. 2 Phonograph invented	

Andersen	Andersen's Works
1878 Christian Andersen resigns from Tivoli Orchestra Joachim Andersen resigns from Royal Orchestra, moves to St. Petersburg Joachim Andersen and Emma Christina Jansson Andersen divorce granted	
1881 Joachim Andersen resigns from St. Petersburg Imperial Orchestra, moves to Berlin	
1882 Joachim Andersen wins position in Berlin Royal Opera orchestra, then within months becomes founding member of Berlin Philharmonic Orchestra	Joachim Andersen performs *Le Carnaval Russe* at Berlin Philharmonic Orchestra's inaugural concert
1883	Taffanel performs op. 3 Taffanel letter mentions op. 5
1884 Joachim Andersen performs Mozart Concerto in D Major, K. 314, on Berlin Philharmonic Orchestra subscription concert End of Bilse Orchestra	
1885 Joachim Andersen appointed assistant conductor of Berlin Philharmonic Orchestra	Op. 21 published Andersen writes dedicatory inscription to Tieftrunk on op. 16
1886	Joachim Andersen performs *Le Carnaval Russe* with Berlin Philharmonic Orchestra
1887	Joachim Andersen performs op. 35 and *Le Carnaval Russe* with Berlin Philharmonic Orchestra

Music Events	World Events
1878 Brahms, Violin Concerto Gilbert and Sullivan, *H. M. S. Pinafore*	Microphone invented
1879 Smetana, *Moldau*	Dostoyevsky, *The Brothers Karamozov*
1881 Boston Symphony Orchestra founded Offenbach, *Tales of Hoffmann*	James, *Portrait of a Lady*
1882 Meiningen Orchestra (conducted by Hans von Bülow) performs in Berlin Berlin Philharmonic Orchestra founded Tchaikovsky, *1812 Overture*	*Berliner Tageblatt* (Berlin newpaper) begins publication Stevenson, *Treasure Island*
1883 Brahms, Symphony No. 3 Metropolitan Opera House opens	Brooklyn Bridge opens
1884 Brahms guest-conducts fledgling Berlin Philharmonic Orchestra	*Politiken* (Copenhagen newspaper) begins publication Twain, *Huckleberry Finn*
1885 First summer season in Scheveningen (Holland) for Berlin Philharmonic Orchestra	
1886 Scheveningen concert hall burns	Nietzsche, *Beyond Good and Evil* Stevenson, *Dr. Jekyll and Mr. Hyde*
1887 Hans von Bülow becomes con- ductor of Berlin Philharmonic Orchestra	

Andersen	Andersen's Works
1888 Joachim Andersen and Carl Esberger perform Saint-Saëns *Tarantella* on Berlin Philharmonic Orchestra subscription concert	Op. 33 published Joachim Andersen performs op. 35 and *Le Carnaval Russe* with Berlin Philharmonic Orchestra
1889 Vigo Andersen granted one-year leave of absence from Royal Orchestra, moves to United States	Publication contract signed with Wilhelm Hansen for op. 37 Joachim Andersen performs *Le Carnaval Russe* with Berlin Philharmonic Orchestra
1890 Vigo Andersen dismissed from Royal Orchestra Sarah Dana Watson begins collecting Joachim Andersen's concert programs and related materials	Joachim Andersen performs op. 35, op. 48, op. 49, and *Le Carnaval Russe* with Berlin Philharmonic Orchestra Joachim Andersen performs op. 28 at a concert of soloists of the Berlin Philharmonic Orchestra
1891 Joachim Andersen marries Sarah Dana Watson Vigo Andersen appointed founding member of Chicago Orchestra Joachim Andersen develops tongue affliction; unable to perform as soloist at Berlin Philharmonic Orchestra concert on December 7	Joachim Andersen performs op. 22, no. 1, op. 24, no. 6, op. 26, op. 35, op. 49, and *Le Carnaval Russe* with Berlin Philharmonic Orchestra
1892 Joachim Andersen's career as performing flutist ends	Franz Schmeling performs op. 35 and *Le Carnaval Russe* with Berlin Philharmonic Orchestra
1893 Joachim Andersen resigns from Berlin Philharmonic Orchestra	Vigo Andersen performs op. 35 with Chicago Orchestra Publication contract signed with Wilhelm Hansen for op. 57 Op. 55, no. 1 and 8, published
1894 Joachim Andersen initiates and conducts a series of concerts in Copenhagen (became known as Palace Concerts in 1895)	Publication contract signed with Wilhelm Hansen for op. 45, op. 50, and op. 58 Op. 46, op. 47, op. 48, op. 55, no. 2-7, and op. 56 published Announcement about impending publication of op. 57

Music Events	World Events

1888 Franck, Symphony in D Minor
Rimsky-Korsakov, *Scheherazade*
	Kaiser Wilhelm II becomes
	  Emperor of Germany
	Jack the Ripper murders six
	  women in London

1889 Dvorak, Symphony No. 8 Mahler, Symphony No. 1 Richard Strauss, *Don Juan*	Motion picture invented Rodin, *The Thinker*
1890 Richard Strauss, *Death and Transfiguration*	Bismarck dismissed by Wilhelm II
1891	Doyle, *Adventures of Sherlock Holmes* Nietzsche, *Thus Spake Zarathustra*

1892 Hans von Bülow's final year
  as Music Director of Berlin
  Philharmonic Orchestra
	Dannebrog (Copenhagen news-
	  paper) begins publication
	Cézanne, *The Card Players*

1893 Taffanel becomes Professor
  of Flute at Paris Conservatory
Dvorak, Symphony, "From the
  New World"
	World's Columbian Exhibition
	  held in Chicago
	Munch, *The Scream*

1894 Debussy, *Prélude à l'après-midi
  d'un faune*
Strauss, *Till Eulenspiegel*
	Alfred Dreyfus Affair begins in
	  France

	Andersen	Andersen's Works

1895	Palace Concert series begins
	Vigo Andersen commits suicide
	Joachim Andersen conducts
	  orchestra at German-Nordic
	  Exhibition of Trade and Indus-
	  try in Lübeck, Germany
		Publication contract signed for
		  op. 59 and op. 61
		Op. 60 published
		Announcement about impending
		  publication of op. 45, op. 50,
		  op. 58, and op. 59
		Request from Taffanel for Andersen
		  to compose op. 61
		Fanny Christensen performs op.
		  59, no. 5, and op. 61 at Lübeck
		  Exhibition

1896	Joachim Andersen founds
	  Orchestra School
		Op. 45 and op. 50 published
		Op. 61 performed by Peter Moller-
		  up at Tivoli Gardens
		Op. 61 performed by Albert
		  Françella and Wilhelm Tieftrunk
		Announcement that op. 59 has
		  been published
		Announcement about impending
		  publication of op. 62

1897	First Orchestra School concert	Andersen writes dedicatory
		  inscription to Sophie
		  Claudius on Sølvmyrter

1898	Joachim Andersen appointed
	  conductor of Tivoli Orchestra
	Joachim Andersen performs on
	  Music History Museum concert
	Joachim Andersen and Schnedler-
	  Petersen engage in dispute
	Caroline Frederikke Andkjær dies
	  Joachim Andersen's mother
		Op. 55, no. 6 and 7, performed by
		  Fanny Christensen at Tivoli
		  Gardens

1899	Christian Andersen dies
	  Joachim Andersen's father
	Ernst Gunner Joachim Andersen
	  dies
	  Joachim Andersen's son
	Joachim Andersen conducts new
	  series of free concerts in
	  Rosenborg Gardens
		Jay Plowe performs op. 54 and op.
		  58 at Tivoli Gardens
		Polonaise composed

Music Events	World Events
1895 Mahler, Symphony No. 2	X-ray invented Yeats, *Poems*
1896 Puccini, *La Bohème*	First modern Olympic Games held in Athens
1897 Georg Lumbye resigns as con- ductor of Tivoli Orchestra (Schnedler-Petersen appointed interim conductor)	
1898 Richard Strauss, *Ein Heldenleben*	Wells, *The War of the Worlds* Shaw, *Caesar and Cleopatra* United States goes to war with Spain Zola, *J'accuse*
1899 Elgar, *Enigma Variations* Joplin, *Maple Leaf Rag* Schoenberg, *Verklärte Nacht* Sibelius, *Finlandia*	First magnetic recording of sound Wilde, *The Importance of Being Earnest*

	Andersen	Andersen's Works
1900		Op. 48 performed at Tivoli Gardens
1901		Emil Prill performs op. 3 and op. 26 at Tivoli Gardens Op. 48 performed by Palace orchestra Theori treatise completed Op. 59, no. 2, performed by Christian Agerup on Orchestra School concert
1902		Op. 48 performed at Tivoli Gardens
1903		Op. 48 performed at Tivoli Gardens
1904	Joachim Andersen visits Taffanel and Paris Conservatory flute class Palace orchestra conflict between Andersen and his musicians	Op. 24, no. 6, and op. 55, no. 5, performed by Johannes Ahlquist on Orchestra School concert Op. 57, no. 3, performed at Tivoli Gardens
1905	Orchestra School moves to Conservatory Joachim Andersen knighted and writes *curriculum vitae* Joachim Andersen appointed to board to examine military bands	Ary van Leeuwen performs op. 16, op. 51, no 2, and op. 55, no. 6, at Tivoli Gardens
1906		Op. 48 performed for benefit concert at Tivoli Gardens Op. 57, no. 3, op. 58, and *Kong Christian X. Honnør-Marsch* performed at Tivoli Gardens *Kong Christian X. Honnør-Marsch* performed at Rosenborg Gardens

Music Events	World Events
1900 Philadelphia Orchestra founded Puccini, *Tosca*	Freud, *The Interpretation of Dreams* Quantum Theory formulated
1901 Mahler, Symphony No. 4 Schoenberg, *Gurrelieder*	Marconi sends trans-Atlantic radio signal First Nobel Prizes awarded
1902 New Tivoli concert hall opens	Conrad, *Heart of Darkness*
1903	Wright brothers' first airplane flights
1904 Puccini, *Madame Butterfly*	Russo-Japanese War begins
1905 Debussy, *La Mer* Richard Strauss, *Salomé*	Einstein's special theory of relativity Rilke, *The Book of Hours*

1906 Mozart Festival begins in
    Salzburg
	King Frederick VIII begins reign in
	    Denmark
	Matisse, *The Joy of Life*

	Andersen	Andersen's Works
1907		Publication contract signed with Wilhelm Hansen for op. 44, op. 62, op. 63, *Kong Christian X. Honnør-Marsch*, *Andante Funebre*, *Einzugsmarsch der Bojaren*, and *Resignation*
Kong Christian X. Honnør-Marsch performed at Tivoli Gardens and Rosenborg Gardens
1908		*Kong Christian X. Honnør-Marsch* performed at Rosenborg Gardens
1909	Joachim Andersen appointed "Professor of Music"
Joachim Andersen conducts his final Palace Concert
Joachim Andersen dies (May 7)	
1910	Sarah Dana Watson Andersen begins work at New York Public Library	
1911		Op. 16 performed at Tivoli Gardens
1912-3	Sarah Dana Watson Andersen donates Joachim Andersen materials to New York Public Library	
1915	Sarah Dana Watson Andersen resigns position at New York Public Library	

Music Events	World Events
1907 First music broadcast	Picasso, *Demoiselles d'Avignon*
1908 Bartók, First String Quartet Hennebains becomes Professor of Flute at Paris Conservatory	
1909 Sergei Diaghilev establishes Ballet Russe in Paris Mahler, Symphony No. 9	Kandinsky's first abstract paintings Frank Lloyd Wright designs Robie House in Chicago NAACP founded
1910 Bartók, *Allegro Barbaro* Ravel, *Daphnis et Chloé* Stravinsky, *The Firebird*	*Dannebrog* (Copenhagen news- paper) ceases publication
1911 Mahler, *Das Lied von der Erde* Strauss, *Der Rosenkavalier*	Lawrence, *The White Peacock*
1912 Schoenberg, *Pierrot Lunaire*	King Christian X begins reign in Denmark *Titanic* sinks
1913 Stravinsky, *Le Sacre du Printemps* Webern, *Six Orchestral Pieces* Scriabin, *Prometheus*	Thomas Mann, *Death in Venice* Proust, *Remembrance of Things Past*
1914 Ives, *Three Places in New England*	World War I begins
1915 Ives, *Concord Sonata*	New Danish Constitution adopted Panama Canal opens
1917 Respighi, *Fountains of Rome*	Russian Revolution Jung, *The Psychology of the Unconscious*

Andersen   Andersen's Works

1928   Last known correspondence of
        Sarah Dana Watson Andersen

1934-5 Robert Enevoldsen sells Joachim
        Andersen's flute to Tivoli
        Gardens

1943   Joachim Andersen's ashes interred
        in Bispebjerg cemetery

Music Events	World Events
1918 Prokofiev, *Classical Symphony* Stravinsky, *L'Histoire du Soldat*	Denmark grants independence to Iceland, though it remained under the Danish king until 1944
1920 Ravel, *La Valse*	North Schleswig returns to Denmark
1921	Joyce, *Ulysses*
1922 Nielsen, Symphony No. 5	Union of Soviet Socialist Republics established
1924 Gershwin, *Rhapsody in Blue*	Stalin becomes dictator of U.S.S.R.
1925 Berg, *Wozzeck*	Kafka, *The Trial*
1928 Gershwin, *An American in Paris*	Penicillin developed Lawrence, *Lady Chatterley's Lover*
1929	New York stock market crash
1931 Palace Concerts end in Copenhagen Varèse, *Ionisation*	Frost, *Collected Poems*
1933	Hitler becomes German Chancellor Reichstag arson
1934 Schnedler-Petersen resigns as conductor of Tivoli Orchestra Hindemith, *Mathis der Maler*	German plebiscite establishes Hitler as Führer
1939 Casino Theater closes in Copenhagen	Germany invades Poland; World War II begins Steinbeck, *The Grapes of Wrath*
1940	Germany occupies Denmark
1941	Japan attacks Pearl Harbor; United States enters World War II
1942	Battle of Stalingrad
1944 Copland, *Appalachian Spring* Bartók, *Concerto for Orchestra*	Berlin "Philharmonie" destroyed Tivoli Gardens bombed Iceland ends union with Denmark, becomes a republic

Index of Musical Compositions

General Index

About the Author

KYLE J. DZAPO is Associate Professor of Music at Bradley University and principal flutist of the Peoria Symphony Orchestra.